Montana and the West Series
Volume V

Battle of the Rosebud:
Prelude to the Little Bighorn

Stylized drawing of General Crook's Battle on the Rosebud depicting the Sioux charging Colonel Royall's detachment of cavalry, June 17, 1876. From *Frank Leslie's Illustrated Newspaper*, Vol. XLII, New York, August 1, 1876, p. 376. by permission of The Huntington Library, San Marino, California

Battle of the Rosebud
Prelude to the Little Bighorn

BY
NEIL C. MANGUM

Neil C Mangum

To Mal Jameson on
the Powder River Campaign
Jan 27, 1998

UPTON & SONS   EL SEGUNDO, CA   1996

———

LIBRARY OF CONGRESS CATALOG CARD NUMBER 87-50694
ISBN 0-912783-11-7
Third printing, 1996

Dust jacket and line drawings by Hank Maynard

DEDICATION
To my parents
Ralph D. Mangum and Nellie H. Mangum
I am eternally grateful

Table of Contents

Illustrations

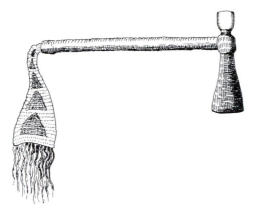

Preface

The battle of the Rosebud represents a strategic victory for the Sioux and Cheyenne against U.S. military troops staged at the zenith of the Sioux War of 1876-1877. In the spring of 1876, three Army columns were placed in the field to force the Indians to submit to reservations. The Indians' victory over Crook effectively neutralized one of the military prongs and enabled the warriors to concentrate on the other two commands. The Indian victory at Rosebud was a prelude to and directly led to a still greater triumph eight days later on June 25, 1876, when Lt. Col. George A. Custer and his immediate command were wiped out to a man by these same warriors who had opposed Crook on the Rosebud. The shocking news of Little Bighorn erased the memories of the Rosebud from all but a few actual battle participants. Yet, it is second only to the Little Bighorn in terms of total number of troops and Indians deployed in battle. Geographically, the Rosebud Battlefield is larger than Custer Battlefield.

Equally significant is the style of fighting exhibited by the Indians. It marked a departure from their customary sporadic hit-and-run tactics. Instead, the Sioux and Cheyenne unified in a common cause, concentrated their forces in large numbers, and fought "with unprecedented group impetuousity." The force under Crook was not prepared for conventional tactics from a heretofore unconventional adversary.

In addition to the historical significance of the site, the land is abundant in archeological extant remains. A 3,500 to 4,000-year old buffalo jump has been excavated. It includes man-made drive lines; 86 piles of rock cairns extend 1,800 feet along the approach to the jump.

My initial visit to Rosebud Battlefield occurred in 1979, shortly after I arrived at my new assignment as chief historian at neighboring Custer Battlefield National Monument. Looking down upon the Rosebud from Crook's Hill left an indelible impression on me. I marveled at the pristine beauty. So natural. Here, on the barren ridge punctuating the battlefield, aided only by the perpetual winds rushing through the short grasses, I pondered the battle, reliving in my mind those thrilling days that make up our American West. I was convinced then that the Rosebud battle was truly a forgotten event and certainly one of the best-kept secrets in all of Montana. Unfortunately, my visit did not include an opportunity to meet with the former landowner of much of the lands comprising the battlefield, Mr. Elmer "Slim" Kobold. Slim was in poor health, waging a personal battle with cancer. A year earlier Slim had experienced a major victory. Putting aside personal monetary gains, Slim had sold his beloved ranch to the State of Montana so that it could be developed into a state monument. He died in 1982.

I returned to the Rosebud on many treks. Armed with J.W. Vaughn's *With Crook at the Rosebud,* my friend, seasonal ranger Gerald Jasmer, and I spent many days debating, discussing, and walking over the battlefield, attempting to delve into its salient features. My interest in the Rosebud fight landed me two tasks with the Montana Fish, Wildlife, and Parks Department, which administers the park. In 1983, I completed a trail guide brochure of the area. Following that, I compiled a "Rosebud Battlefield Historic Base Data Study" in 1984. I owe a great debt of gratitude to Dave Conklin, Doug Monger, and Randy Wuertz, state park employees, who encouraged me to conduct the research.

Others deserve mentioning, too. Preeminent is Richard Upton, El Segundo, California, who approached me to turn my history study into a book. Paul L. Hedren, Superintendent, Fort Union Trading Post National Historic Site, North Dakota; Joseph C. Porter, Curator of Western American History and Ethnology in the Center for Western Studies, Joslyn Art Museum, Omaha, Nebraska; Jerome Greene, Staff Historian, Denver Service Center, National Park Service, Denver, Colorado; B. William Henry, Historian, Jefferson National Expansion Memorial, St. Louis, Missouri; Gary Howe, Superintendent, Fort Laramie National Historic Site, Wyoming; Father Barry Hagen, Archivist, University of Portland; George Mathews, seasonal ranger, who willingly supplied me with the map of the Prairie Dog Creek fight, and William Schultz who drew the Rosebud Battlefield base map.

Several public repositories aided my search. They include: University of Oregon, Hilary Cummings, Curator of Manuscripts, Library; U.S. Army Military History Institute, Carlisle Barracks, Richard J. Sommers, Archivist-Historian; Coe Library, University of Wyoming; Colorado State Historical Society, Denver, Colorado; University of Oklahoma Press, Norman; United States Military Academy, Marie T. Capps, Maps and Manuscripts Librarian; and the National Archives, Washington, D.C.

No book of mine is complete until I pay the highest tribute to a devoted wife and daughters who painstakingly at times allowed me to climb my mountain.

Battle of the Rosebud:
Prelude to the Little Bighorn

CHAPTER I

Fizzle on Powder River

The sound of crunching snow impacting under the weight of a thousand horses' hooves reverberated against the steep canyon walls ensconcing Powder River Valley. At a brisk walk rode six companies of the 2nd and 3rd U.S. Cavalry. A glassy-eyed stare was the only countenance on most of the soldier's stoic faces, a condition manifested by prolonged exposure to subzero temperatures and the unlimited expanse of Montana, now coated in a blinding canopy of white. Snake-like, the column plodded up the valley, crossing and recrossing the river on a firm bed of ice. After sunset the weary men reached Lodgepole Creek [Clear Creek] at a point just inside the present boundary of Wyoming. It was here, on Clear Creek, that the anticipated rendezvous with General George Crook was supposed to materialize. But Crook was nowhere to be found. The command pushed on for another two miles, finally halting in a large open area which afforded some grazing for the jaded animals.

The men and animals had been pushed to the brink of physical endurance. They had marched 54 miles in 24 hours, with no rest for the past 36, and had fought a four-hour battle, subsisting on nothing more than one frigid meal of hardtack.[1] Lieutenant John G. Bourke, aide to Crook, who accompanied Reynolds, appropriately dubbed their bleak bivouac "Camp Inhospitality." Bourke noted in his diary, "There was a sufficiency of water or ice

— enough wood ... There was nothing to eat; not even for the wounded men ..."[2] Mental fatigue and numbness from the freezing elements gnawed at the core of the trooper's senses. But even this material factor was secondary. With little exception, most of the men were encountering flashbacks of the day's events. That morning, March 17, 1876, they had been engaged in an attack on a sleeping Indian village of 105 lodges, a village composed chiefly of Cheyennes and a few Sioux.

The day before, near Otter Creek, Crook's scouts had located two Indians trailing game tracks. Keeping at a safe distance, scout Frank Grouard watched them until he was satisfied they were heading toward their camp, which seemed to be in the direction of Powder River.[3] General Crook tendered to Colonel Joseph J. Reynolds, the white-haired commander of the Third Cavalry, the option of remaining with the pack train or spearheading the attack.[4] As if there really were any decision to be made, Reynolds obviously elected to command the latter. Crook informed Reynolds that he was to take six companies of cavalry, four of the 3rd and two of the 2nd, a total of 15 officers and 359 enlisted men. Reynolds was ordered to strike the Indians, inflicting as much damage as possible. Crook wanted the accomplishment to include capturing the pony herd and bringing away with him meat and other provisions which, in turn, could be utilized by the entire command to sustain themselves in the field should further operations be warranted.[5] Taking the remaining four companies of cavalry along with the pack train, Crook would rejoin Reynolds on Clear Creek on the evening of the 17th.

The assault on the village would necessitate a cavalryman's bane, a night march. Breaking camp about dusk, the cavalcade swung into cold saddles. Their route was up the north fork of Otter Creek. Pervasive winds whipped snow into the eyes and burned the skin of the men. Still worse, the men had to grope their way over icy ridges and snow-filled ravines, without benefit of illumination. A layer of clouds concealed any light the moon might have provided. The ordeal was particularly hard on the mounts, who had to plunge and pull through the deep snows. This further but necessary exertion by the horses served to deplete their energy reserves, already dangerously low from the rigors of the campaign, now entering its 17th day.

Before dawn Reynolds reached the bluffs west of Powder River. Below him, in the valley and situated along the left bank of the stream, lay his objective. Luck was on the side of the cavalry. From all appearances, the encamped Indians were not aware of any impending danger. Once again the Indians were in an unenviable position — having to pay the price for not properly posting guards to alert the village to danger. This raw March morning found them asleep in their lodges. Meanwhile, Reynolds surreptitiously made plans to attack. Reynolds' strategy was bold and tactically sound. His cavalry would converge from the north, west, and south.

Victory should have been complete. It was not. The charge was scheduled to begin at about 7:30 A.M., with the first gray streaks of dawn emerging on the eastern horizon. However, Reynolds experienced aggravating delays brought on because of rough terrain and circuitous routes traveled to place the men into position.[6] It was fully 9 A.M. before the opening salvos emanating from the reports of Army Colt .45s belonging to Captain James "Teddy" Egan's Company K, 2nd Cavalry, signaled that the battle was underway.[7]

Initially the action went favorably for the bluecoats. Egan's charge, supported by Captain Anson Mills' battalion, routed the unsuspecting villagers, putting them to flight. In all, about 200 warriors occupied the village of 700 inhabitants. Most of the warriors were Cheyennes under Old Bear and Little Wolf, but among them were a few Minneconjou and Oglala Sioux. Captain Alexander Moore's battalion was supposed to have taken a position north of the camp to preclude the escape of Indians in that direction. However, Moore was unable to fulfill his objective, and most of the warriors and villagers scattered northward, leaving the empty encampment in the hands of Egan and Mills.

Shortly after Egan and Mills' charge, Colonel Reynolds entered the village to examine his prize. He found more than a hundred lodges, tons of dried buffalo meat and robes, other food sources, and vast quantities of ammunition. Reynolds interrogated an aged Indian woman suffering from a bullet wound in the thigh. She reported that the camp had been Cheyenne but included Oglalas, including Crazy Horse, thus giving rise to the story that Crazy Horse was present.[8] However, ample evidence in the form of direct Indian testimony indicated Crazy Horse was not there. Instead, he was wintering some 60 miles downstream and to the east along Little Powder River.[9]

What to do with the captured village became Reynolds' paramount concern. Crook's instructions had been quite specific — seize all food and bring it off for future consumption by the army. Reynolds elected not to do so, and he explained his motives more fully at his subsequent court-martial declaring:

> I presumed as a matter of course that there must be considerable property in a village of this size, but as it was wholly impractical for me to transport it I determined to destroy everything that we could lay our hands on and then resume the march up the river to meet the other portion of the command at the mouth of Lodgepole [Clear Creek] according to agreement.[10]

At the time Reynolds made the decision to burn the village and all the camp impedimenta, his column was not under immediate threat. Convincing himself he had accomplished all that was expected of him, he commenced at about 11 A.M. to torch everything. He pondered that the more he lingered, the greater the chance of dilution of his achievements.

While Reynolds was engaged in destroying the contents of the village, warriors began assembling on the bluffs west of camp. To make matters worse, some Indians were noticed infiltrating the brush paralleling the river bank, which afforded excellent coverage and concealment. Another cause for alarm was the status of the led horses. They were still on the bluffs to the west. Something would have to be done soon to prevent their capture by warriors seen making their way along the slopes north of the village.[11]

With the contents of the village engulfed in a pall of black smoke, naked warriors, their battle ardor increased at the sight of their former homes going up in flames, began to exert pressure on Reynolds' line. Reynolds' position resembled an inverted "U" with the loop of the "U" running across the Indian camp.[12] Mills' battalion anchored the center of the area forming the base of the "U". To his right came Egan's men who protected the right flank fixed alongside the river. Captain Moore's battalion rested on the left, underneath a mesa which extended about 600 yards westward to meet the base of the bluffs where the Indians were now concentrating. From these dominant ridges Indians poured in a distracting fire which drove Moore further beneath the shelf of the mesa. Moore's retreat left a 150-yard gap between his men and Mills. Warriors along the bank of the Powder began to fire on Egan, which drove him from his ground too, leaving Mills with no friends on either flank.

A worried and excitable Mills went directly to Reynolds to request support.[13] He pleaded with his commander that if Egan and Moore did not firm up, he would be forced to withdraw. Reynolds soon demonstrated that he clearly had no intentions of remaining in the camp and giving the Indians battle. He had already issued orders for the led horses to be brought up in preparation for abandoning the site. In pure and simple terms, Reynolds allowed the Indians to regain the initiative, a dangerous set of circumstances under any military act. To support Mills, Captain Noyes, commanding Company I, 2nd Cavalry, was ordered forward to assist in the withdrawal. Incredible as it may sound, Noyes' company had been allowed to sit idle during the fighting. The commander at the start of the battle had cut out a pony herd, took them to the rear, and then permitted his men to dismount, unsaddle their horses, and boil coffee.[14] A messenger reached Noyes around noon with word to bring his company forward. It took about an hour for Noyes to comply, arriving on the line at 1 P.M.[15]

With Noyes up, Egan and Mills withdrew their men from the skirmish line and began to retire upstream for the prearranged meeting with Crook and the supply train. It was 1:30 P.M. The battle was over. Observing the soldiers' withdrawal, warriors pursued closely. In fact Reynolds' retreat from the village had been so precipitous that in the confusion several of the wounded and dead fell into the possession of the Indians. Ugly rumors ran rampant concerning abandonment of the wounded. Unflattering remarks about Reynolds were made between various officers and among the enlisted personnel. Overall, casualties amounted to four killed and six wounded. Indian losses are unknown, but according to one account, only one warrior was killed.

The troopers attempted to make the best of a dreary evening at "Camp Inhospitality." Bourke continued his tirade of the miserable conditions in camp by recording, "Here and there would be found a soldier, or officer, or scout who had carried a handful of cracker-crumbs in his saddlebags, another who had had the good sense to pick up a piece of buffalo meat in the village, or a third who could produce a spoonful of coffee."[16]

An Indian pony herd numbering 700 animals was driven with the command. Out of compassion for the exhausted men, Reynolds posted only a token force to guard the herd.[17] The next morning the stealth of the Indians paid big dividends, for the pony herd was missing, the last vestiges of it seen crossing the bluffs and headed down the valley. Officers urged Reynolds to dispatch a party out after it, but he declined, declaring, "I deemed it inadvisable in the condition of our horses to attempt a long and doubtful chase after the ponies."[18] This final act of omission uncorked the temper of some of the officers. An outraged Bourke noted this "exhibition of incompetency was the last link needed to fasten the chain of popular obloquy to the reputation of our Commanding Officer."[19]

The whereabouts of Crook was more disconcerting to Reynolds than the recapture of a few brood mares and foals. A vacillating Reynolds pondered his quandary. Out of provisions and with Crook long overdue, he finally settled on a new course of action. Scouts were to make a search for the General. Meanwhile the battalion commanders were to prepare their men to break camp. Reynolds would not wait any longer for Crook. Instead they would return to the supply base located at old Fort Reno, 100 miles to the south.

While the camp was preparing to move out, Crook finally showed up around noon. Crook blamed his tardiness on the fact he had misjudged the distance to Clear Creek. Initially Crook offered congratulatory plaudits to Reynolds, but they soon turned to bitter recriminations. It was apparent the expedition had failed in its objective to subdue the truculent Sioux and Cheyenne. Returning to Fort Fetterman on March 26, Crook promptly preferred charges against Reynolds for destroying the much needed supplies, abandoning the wounded, and permitting the recapture of the pony herd. In turn the domino theory prevailed. Colonel Reynolds preferred charges against Captain Moore and Noyes. Noyes was accused of negligence for allowing his men to unsaddle in the face of the enemy. Moore was charged with not fully cooperating in the attack, an accusation that carried implications of cowardice. With the exception of Noyes' trial, which was held at Fort D.A. Russell in April 1876, repeated delays would postpone Reynolds' and Moore's court-martials until January 1877.[20]

The trial of Colonel Reynolds was bitter and long. In the end he was found guilty along with Moore. Both were given suspensions. President Grant interceded in their behalf, taking into account their previous military records. Grant remitted their sentences. The damage was done however. Powder River ruined their careers. Reynolds resigned in 1877, Moore two years later. In the case of Captain Noyes, that officer freely admitted to the charges but insisted in his trial "that the action was a small skirmish at long range and could not be dignified by the term 'battle.'".[21] The court's findings found Noyes guilty of an "error in judgment." He received an official reprimand.

One must wonder had the soldiers fought as hard against the Sioux and Cheyenne as they did with each other during the court-martial proceedings, whether the results of Crook's Powder River Campaign could have been different. Furthermore, the allegations completely disrupted the officer corps of the Third and to some degree influenced their personal feelings toward Crook.

The Powder River fight was a fizzle. General Philip Sheridan's worst fears of the Indians eluding the Army were realized. The only thing left to do was to organize a new offensive and wait for the spring thaws to launch a punitive expedition. The situation the Army would encounter then would be different. No longer would isolated Indian camps be found and easily beaten in detail. The fight on March 17 gave clear, concise warning to the non-reservation Indians that the Army meant business.

The Powder River experience emboldened the Indians to think and act differently. Safety lay in numbers, and they began to band together. Resolute in their will, strong in their determination to retain their lands, they prepared themselves for the ultimate task of defending their homes. Seeds of disaster sown by the Army on Powder River would ripen on a creek named Rosebud and bear a bountiful harvest later on the Little Bighorn. George Crook would need time to reorganize and prepare a larger army to accomplish the government's ultimatum: the time had come for recalcitrant Sioux and Cheyennes to report to reservations.

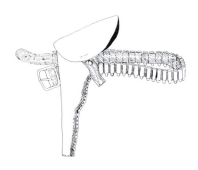

CHAPTER II

The Making of George Crook

General Crook returned to Omaha, headquarters for his Department of the Platte. His department embraced the present states of Iowa, Nebraska, Wyoming, Utah, and a small corner of southern Idaho.[1] In the centennial year of the United States, Crook was perceived almost universally as a solid, dependable soldier. The public, and to a large extent the hierarchy of the Army high command, considered him one of the more talented of a large cadre of successful Civil War generals turned Indian War fighters.

The gray-eyed, bearded Ohioan was born near Dayton September 8, 1828. Crook was number nine of 10 children born to Thomas and Elizabeth Crook. In 1848 he was appointed to the United States Military Academy by a Whig Congressman, Robert P. Schenck, to fill a vacancy in the Third Congressional District of Ohio.[2] In later years Schenck recalled that the boy was reticent to the point of being non-communicative, but otherwise seemed to be of West Point quality.[3] Crook's taciturn demeanor would be a hallmark characteristic that would footnote his entire life.

Cadet Crook was no scholar, for he habitually floundered near the bottom of his class standings. He neutralized his academic deficiencies by at least displaying a penchant for avoiding demerits. Never a heavy socializer and being naturally silent, he refrained from joining the other cadets in getting into mischief. The West Point order and letter books reveal that he received only a few demerits for his five years at the Academy. Crook graduated from West Point in 1852, 38th out of a class of 43.[4] Crook has the distinction of being the lowest ranking cadet ever to earn a major general's insignia in the United States Army.[5]

Among his classmates was Philip H. Sheridan, who in 1876 was Crook's immediate superior, commanding the Division of the Missouri. Sheridan's vast domain stretched from the Canadian line to the border of Mexico. Crook's association with Sheridan continued after West Point, when they were both assigned to frontier stations in the Pacific Northwest. Crook's first assignment was in northern California where he was attached to the 4th Infantry as a newly commissioned brevet 2nd Lieutenant in Company F. After a brief stint in California, his company was transferred to Oregon and Washington.

During the Rogue River War in Oregon he received a painful arrow wound in the right hip. When he attempted to remove the arrow, the head remained. Crook recovered, but he carried the arrow point in his hip the remainder of his life.[6] In 1857 he was promoted to First Lieutenant and reassigned to Company D, 4th Infantry.

At the outset of the Civil War, Crook used his political influence to gain a colonelcy in the 36th Ohio Volunteers. He went to Schenck, who had promoted his appointment to West Point, and to Governor Dennison of Ohio to secure the position.

Detailed to West Virginia, he earned valuable experience in subsequent expeditions. While stationed at Lewisburg, he was given a provisional brigade consisting of his regiment, the 44th Ohio, and the 2nd West Virginia Cavalry. He gained his first combat honors on May 23, 1862, when his brigade drove a Confederate force under General Henry Heth out of Lewisburg with severe losses. For his conduct Crook was brevetted Major for gallant and meritorius service at Lewisburg.[7]

Later that summer Crook assumed command of a brigade consisting of his own 36th Ohio and three other Buckeye regiments.[8] Crook's brigade was successful in clearing Confederate units from a large region of western Virginia. More importantly, Crook was appointed Brigadier General to date from September 7, although not confirmed until October 1.[9]

Confederate successes in eastern Virginia dictated the transfer of units from West Virginia. In late August Crook's force became attached to major operations around Washington D.C. In advance of his brigade, Crook and the 36th Ohio were temporarily attached to General John Pope, acting as a bodyguard.[10] Crook witnessed the utter rout of Union forces at Second Manassas. His 36th Ohio was detailed to pick up stragglers, and before long, Crook had rounded up 15,000 disorganized refugees from Pope's shattered Army.[11]

During the Maryland Campaign, Crook's brigade formed part of General Ambrose E. Burnside's 9th Army Corps.[12] The sanguinary engagement at South Mountain, September 14, 1862, was duplicated three days later with devastating carnage at the Battle of Antietam (Sharpsburg). As part of Burnside's Corps, Crook found his brigade fighting for control of Burnside Bridge. Ultimately Federal forces were able to turn the Confederate right at Antietam. Had it not been for the timely arrival of A.P. Hill's Confederate Division advancing on Sharpsburg, Crook might have basked in the glory of seeing the destruction of the better part of Robert E. Lee's forces.

In October Crook found that his promotion to Brigadier General had been confirmed. He returned to the Kanawha District to superintend affairs there. His major thrust was to minimize the activities of bushwhackers and partisan rangers.[13]

At the beginning of 1863, Crook was transferred to the western theater. He was placed in command of a cavalry division in George H. Thomas' Army of the Cumberland. In September Crook's cavalry was engaged in spirited actions involving the

Union withdrawal at the Battle of Chickamauga. Crook returned to West Virginia in January, again as commander of the Kanawha District. Crook's West Virginia force was given a significant role in General Grant's strategy to exert pressure on the Confederacy at every point. General Grant summoned Crook to his head-quarters at Spotsylvania Court House in the spring. The conversation dealt with Crook's mission in Grant's overall strangle-hold on the Confederates.

Grant ordered Crook to raid south from Charleston into western Virginia. His goal was to strike the Virginia and Tennessee Railroad, tear up track and destroy the bridge over the New River. If successful in that enterprise, he was to follow the tracks northeast and link up with General Franz Sigel for a planned capture of Lynchburg.[14]

Crook made the most of his independent command. Leading a force of nearly 8,000 men, he advanced from south central West Virginia into Virginia. On May 9, he met and defeated an inferior array of Confederates at Cloyd's Mountain near Dublin, Virginia. The Confederate commander, Albert Jenkins, was mortally wounded in the fight. Rutherford B. Hayes, the future President, maintained a diary and recounted his admiration for Crook. Hayes wrote that Crook had led the fight in person and was the finest general he had seen since the war, except Rosecrans.[15]

Crook pursued the retreating Rebels but was unable to bring them to battle. Crook encountered little difficulty in executing the first part of Grant's desires. The tracks of the Virginia and Tennessee Railroad were rendered a twisted ribbon of steel, while the strategically important bridge over New River was reduced to a smoldering, blackened ruin. The second phase of the operations — to unite with Sigel on the reduction of Lynch-burg — was abortive, although no culpability was attached to Crook's part. Hitting the railroad, Crook turned north, following the tracks. He advanced as far as Christiansburg before turning back and retiring on his supply line. In his autobiography Crook stated the reasons he fell back were fear for Confederate reinforcements thought to be enroute, and the lack of any intelligence from General Sigel.[16] Crook was unaware that on May 15, Sigel had been utterly routed by a Confederate force at New Market in the lower Shenandoah Valley. Crook summarily fell back on his headquarters at Meadow Bluff.

The new commander in the area, Major General David Hunter, sent Crook orders to join him at Staunton, where they would move on Lynchburg. Hunter's advance on Lynchburg went without a hitch until it reached the outskirts of the city. Robert E. Lee had dispatched Jubal Early's Second Corps to blunt the Federal advance. Arriving in the nick of time, Early's butternuts drove the Union soldiers in disorder from the town and back into West Virginia. Most of the time Crook's Division was posted as rear guard, where much of the fighting occurred. Although Hunter retreated to Charleston with the campaign ending in disgrace, Crook was highly praised for the efficient and professional manner in which he handled his men.[17]

Crook's military star was rising. For his skills and abilities displayed in Hunter's abortive campaign to take Lynchburg, Crook was given the Department of West Virginia. He had little opportunity to do anything in his department because Jubal Early was threatening the Capitol. General Grant dispatched General Sheridan to the Shenandoah Valley to stymie Early and ostensibly to drive him from the region for good. Sheridan established headquarters in Harpers Ferry and augmented his army by attaching Crook's department to his newly created Army of the Shenandoah. Glad to have his old friend Crook, Sheridan expressed confidence in Crook's qualifications and performances as a general.[18] Coinciding with his reunion with Sheridan was his promotion to Major General.

In the battles of Winchester (September 19) and Fisher's Hill (September 22), Crook's force was the hammer blow of Little

Phil's attack. In both instances Crook's two divisions, now designated the 8th Army Corps, turned the Confederate left flank and put Jubal Early's overmatched army to precipitous flight. Winchester and Fisher's Hill marked the high point of Crook's Civil War career. But fate is fickle. Crook, the shining star of Sheridan's command was about to turn into a plummeting comet. A month later Crook's reputation was severely stung.

On October 19, his corps anchored the Union left flank along Cedar Creek, a few miles south of Winchester. Perhaps the success had spawned overconfidence, for Crook failed to post sufficient pickets along the sluggish stream.

In a bold and daring move, the Confederates stole a march on the Federals and surprised Crook's corps in a dawn attack. Crook's men were routed. In vain he endeavored to halt the flight, but he was powerless to stop it. The rout was infectious, spilling over to part of two other corps. Sheridan, who had been in Winchester, hurried to the sound of the guns. By late afternoon Sheridan's charismatic personality had restored a semblance of order to his stricken command. With the punch gone from the Confederate attack, Sheridan unleashed his infantry and cavalry in a counterattack that rolled over Early's beleaguered and hapless force.[19]

Cedar Creek decimated Crook, and fractured his personal relationship with Sheridan. Embittered by the accolades with which the press was showering Sheridan, and perhaps smarting from his own failures at Cedar Creek, Crook from that day forward became an outspoken critic of his onetime friend. Sheridan attempted to console his wounded pride following Cedar Creek by declaring, "Crook, I am going to get much more credit for this than I deserve, for, had I been here in the morning the same thing would have taken place."[20] But Crook would never forget, and in the process forged a wedge of discontent between the two that would last the rest of their lives. Much has been written of the ambitious Nelson A. Miles and George A.

Custer, and of their blatant self-aggrandizing. Crook was just as ambitious, although writers have regarded him as humble. The major difference was that Crook concealed from view his burning desire for promotions.[21]

Cedar Creek marks the decline of Crook's Civil War career. From that point on his path followed a decidedly downward trend. It was punctuated with relatively minor roles in the drama but did include one more personal embarrassment.

With Confederate resistance non-extant in the Shenandoah region, Crook was free to return to his departmental command in West Virginia. In February 1865, he suffered the inglorious when he was rousted from his bed at the Dover House in Cumberland, Maryland, by partisan rangers. Rangers, donning Union uniforms, had gotten by the pickets and entered the town, which was surrounded by neary 10,000 of Crook's men.[22] He was taken captive and sent to Richmond's Libby Prison. He spent several weeks there before he was paroled.[23]

Now that Crook was back behind Union lines, General Grant gave him a new position, that of the commander of the cavalry of the Army of the Potomac. Unfortunately for Crook, the war drew to a close before he could become engaged in any of the important actions terminating hostilities.

George Crook emerged from the Civil War a major general of volunteers. His regular army rank, however, had only progressed to that of captain. Reorganization of the military in 1866 produced a few more regiments. He was offered the appointment to the lieutenant colonelcy of the 22nd Infantry which he accepted. Crook returned to the West, where he had been before the Civil War. And there he would serve until nearly the end of his career and death in 1890.

Crook's first assignment in 1866 placed him in command of Fort Boise, Idaho. He quickly excelled in his new duties. Aggressive and tenacious, he earned the watchfulness of his superiors. He adroitly brought under control the Pauites of southern Idaho. In appreciation of his fine effort, he was rewarded with the command of the Department of the Columbia.[24]

He was transferred to the Southwest, when conflicts with Apaches erupted. In 1872-1873, he culminated a brillant campaign along the Tonto Basin. Part of Crook's success was his ability to utilize Indians to catch Indians. He also appreciated the value and the mobiity of pack trains. Carrying much of his supplies on packs enabled Crook to stay in the field and wear down his opponent.

Crook's military star was on the rise again. Superiors interceded in his behalf and garnered him a brigadier's commission. In receiving this promotion he leapfrogged completely past the rank of colonel. His promotion did not follow the normal seniority-conscious military and produced enmities within the officer corps of the Army.

Growing strife on the Northern Plains in 1875 was the major reason Crook was transferred to the Department of the Platte, with headquarters in Omaha. Because of his proven reputation, Western papers quite naturally held him in high esteem. Even the dismal winter campaign on Powder River did nothing to tarnish his rapport with newspapermen. Following the debacle on Powder River, the *Cheyenne Daily Leader* reported, "General Crook is too good and too brave . . . If the soldiers will stick by him, he will stick by them, and the whole command will either conquer or fall together."[25]

At the outset of his May expedition, General Crook was 47 years old. He was six feet tall, of medium build, with broad shoulders and straight as an arrow. A gray beard with elongated points concealed an angular jaw. Penetrating gray eyes emphasized a countenance of savy determination to excel in whatever mission he was entrusted with. Somewhat of an eccentric, he took to riding a mule. Like many frontier officers, he disdained official attire, selecting instead to adorn himself in simple habiliments. During the Apache campaign, he dressed in a canvas hunting suit and pith helmet.[26] During the Sioux wars, he switched to a private's uniform and overcoat with a high crowned black hat.

From Omaha in April, Crook began to mobilize a much larger army for the task of forcing Indians to accept life on reservations. Overall his command would comprise one of three military columns placed in the field in 1876. General Sheridan from his divisional headquarters in Chicago organized operations to ferret out the recalcitrant Indians, who would be found in their usual haunts, the unceded Indian country. This vast tract of real estate encompassed the northeastern portion of Wyoming and the southeastern region of Montana.

The first prong to get underway was the column under Colonel John Gibbon. Leaving Fort Ellis, near Bozeman, Montana, Gibbon's contingent of 450 men, consisting of six companies of the 7th Infantry and four companies of the 2nd Cavalry, patrolled eastward along the Yellowstone River. Gibbon was ordered to proceed along the north bank of the Yellowstone and preclude the escape of Indians across the Yellowstone. This maneuver would prevent Indians from gaining access to the interior of Montana and head off any possible escape to Canada.[27]

The second arm of the three-prong advance originated from Fort Abraham Lincoln. Lincoln was situated on the right bank of the Missouri River, across from the boom town of Bismarck, Dakota Territory. Its commander was General Alfred H. Terry. The column consisted of just under 1,000 men. The bulk of Terry's strike force was the 7th Cavalry, whose commander was the capable if supremely egotistical George Armstrong Custer. At Terry's disposal were the 12 companies of the 7th and three infantry companies, two from the 17th Infantry and one from the 6th. The Dakota Column, as it was formerly dubbed, departed Fort Lincoln on May 17. Their trek would take them westward across the plains of Dakota and Montana Territories.

With the use of the natural highways, the Missouri and Yellowstone rivers, Terry hoped to maintain an open line of communication with Gibbon, who was in his department and reported directly to Terry. That could not be said of Crook, who was in his own department and answered directly to Sheridan. Communications between Terry and Crook would entail difficult if not unsolvable problems. To communicate with Terry would require Crook to dispatch a courier from his position and send him to Fort Fetterman, Wyoming. From Fetterman a telegraph operator could tap out a message and send it along the wires to Omaha, departmental headquarters. From that point the message would be relayed to divisional headquarters in Chicago. In turn staff officers would send the message on to Terry's headquarters in St. Paul. From there the message would be sent to Bismarck, at the terminus of the telegraph system in 1876. The message then would be placed on board one of the steamboats contracted by the government to ferry supplies and goods up the Missouri and Yellowstone. Terry had an advanced supply depot established at the mouth of Glendive Creek on the Yellowstone. Once the message got to that point, it would be taken overland by courier to Terry in the field. With good fortune, the exchange of information would necessitate about two weeks to complete. The reverse of this scenario would take place too, should Terry initiate communication. Needless to say, when both columns entered the field, messages would be kept to a minimum until close approximation of the two columns was known. As events turned out, this antiquated relay system never materialized

By mid-May Crook began to concentrate his forces at Fort Fetterman, about 90 miles northwest of Fort Laramie, Wyoming. Crook would command the third wing of the pincer-like movement. His mission was to march northward and, in conjunction with Terry, try to find the Indians, defeat them in battle, or, at the very least, force them to fall into the hands of one of the other two converging columns. However, it should be pointed out, no official action was planned whereby all three columns would act in such close concert as to be able to attack simultaneously.[28] The area was too large, and the migratory patterning of the Indians, unpredictable. Thus any one of the three columns was considered strong enough to defend itself and certainly strong enough to deal with whatever force of Indians it might encounter. To compound the matter, the entire campaign was predicated on soon-to-prove-faulty information, that the Indians would attempt to elude the Army rather than stand and fight. Gathering intelligence information from the Indian Bureau, the army estimated that no more than 500-800 warriors were absent from the reservations.[29] As things turned out, the Indians achieved a fighting force of between 2000 and 4000 for a short time during the summer. Crook at Rosebud was to meet in battle about 1,500, while the unlucky Custer slammed into almost twice as many.

The bottom line of the military thinking was not the strength of the Indians, but the Army's concern with bringing them to bay. The attention of the military was on preventing the Indians from escaping. If the three columns could maneuver the Indians into the path of another column, the army then stood a fair chance of inflicting heavy casualties on the Indians and thereby inducing them to surrender.

Officers and men were painfully aware that most Indian campaigns in the summer resulted in few pitched battles and were usually reduced to nothing more than futile chases. Moreover, the Indians seldom fought against large concentrations of bluecoated soldiers, preferring instead to disassemble their villages and scatter over the countryside. Military minds had every right to expect, based on previous experience, that any formidable bands of Sioux could not be kept together for a sustained period of time in a central location because of grass and game depletion.[30]

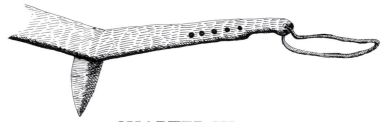

CHAPTER III

The Big Horn and Yellowstone Expedition

Crook waged an unrelenting campaign from Omaha to prepare his department for readiness. Additional troops were brought in from other departments, and garrisons within his command were stripped for field operations. Crook concentrated troops at three posts in preparation for the summer expedition. Soldiers massed at Fort D.A. Russell, near Cheyenne, at Fort Laramie, and Fort Fetterman.

While subordinates were busy shuffling troops and outfitting the expedition with supplies, Crook was engaged in other logistical problems within his department. Of particular concern were the mounting troubles involving marauding Indians in Wyoming and western Nebraska. Governor John M. Thayer of Wyoming telegraphed Crook on April 24, 1876, requesting military assistance. The road connecting Fort Laramie and Custer City had become a haven for Indians and outlaws who had committed a series of brutal murders. Crook gave the matter his personal attention. Taking the train to Cheyenne, Crook assured the governor and the press that troops would patrol the area and provide "perfect security."[1]

Other crises emerged requiring the general's attention. Crook, who was a sympathetic supporter of Indian rights, was appalled at the deplorable conditions confronting Indians on the Red Cloud and Spotted Tail Agencies. Lieutenant Colonel Luther

Bradley reported to Crook from Fort Laramie that the Sioux were suffering from lack of food. Crook, always quick to act, wired General Sheridan in Chicago and warned that unless Indians at the agencies were supplied with adequate provisions — for nothing more than survival — they would be compelled to leave the reservations and join up with the hostile elements. Crook fretted. He and Sheridan were powerless to be anything more than compassionate pawns in the plight of the Indians. The issuance of provisions to the Indians was under the jurisdiction of the Indian Bureau, U.S. Department of the Interior. It was not the responsibility of the Army.[2] Crook knew full well that a number of warriors, if not a majority, would defect to the Powder River Country, rendering his job all the more difficult.

As he had done for his March expedition, Crook designated Fort Fetterman the assembly and jumping-off point for the Big Horn Expedition. Fetterman was located about 10 miles northwest of present-day Douglas, Wyoming. The post was considered one of the less desirable assignments in the Army. It was a desolate duty station far removed from the treats of civilization. The surrounding terrain was distinguished by the absence of trees or any other redeeming features save perhaps the local hog ranch located just outside the military reservation. The post had been named in honor of Captain William J. Fetterman, who had been killed along with his entire command of 80 men near Fort Phil Kearny on December 21, 1866. But now in the spring of 1876, the unpopular fort was bristling with activity. At Fetterman, Crook stockpiled a mountain of supplies necessary to keep his command in the field. Present or enroute were 300,000 pounds of grain, thousands of pounds of pork, beans, coffee, and sugar. Crates of ammunition, hundreds of wagons and a beef herd of more than 1,200 rounded out the essentials required to keep an army of over 1,000 in the field.[3]

On May 9, Crook and his aide, Lieutenant John G. Bourke, departed Omaha to take command of the expedition. Stopping first in Cheyenne, they met briefly with some of the officers of the Third Cavalry. Following the Powder River fight, dissention, in which Crook played a large part, had permeated the ranks of the Third Cavalry. Delays had postponed Reynolds' and Moore's court-martials, leaving those two officers in limbo for the forthcoming campaign and still under arrest.

Finishing business in Cheyenne, Crook proceeded to Camp Robinson and Red Cloud Agency. There he hoped to enlist the services of Sioux as scouts. Crook, a proponent of using Indians to catch Indians, met with Agent Hastings to discuss the employment of scouts. Hastings was cool to Crook's idea, perhaps as a result of Crook's report following the March 17 fight. In that communique Crook maintained that large amounts of ammunition found in the Cheyenne village had originated from the Red Cloud Agency.[4] The unsupportive Hastings gave Crook approval to talk to leading Sioux statesmen but went on record as personally discouraging any Indians from participating in the campaign.[5]

Crook conferred with Red Cloud. The haughty chief informed him:

> The Gray Fox must understand that the Dakotas and especially the Oga al la-las [*sic*] have many warriors, many guns and ponies. They are brave and ready to fight for their country. They are not afraid of the soldiers nor of their chief. Many braves are ready to meet them. Every lodge will send its young men, and they all will say of the Great Father's dogs, "Let them come!"[6]

Not one Sioux joined Crook. A bitter Bourke claimed that Hastings had forbidden any Sioux from joining the expedition.[7]

Returning to Fort Laramie, the general received a telegram from Sheridan indicating the Dakota Column had left Fort Abraham Lincoln on the 16th (actually on the 17th). At last report the malcontents were believed to be still on the Little Missouri or its tributaries. According to sources, the non-reservation Indians had 1,500 lodges. Sheridan urged Crook to get underway as quickly as possible.[8] Wasting little time, he departed for Fort Fetterman on the 18th.

Crook assumed official command of the column on May 29. The expedition was commonly referred to as the Big Horn and Yellowstone Expedition. General Orders Number One placed Lieutenant Colonel William B. Royall, the "tall handsome Virginian," in command of all the cavalry. Major Alexander W. Evans commanded the ten companies of the Third Cavalry, while Captain Henry Noyes took charge of the five companies of the Second Cavalry.[9] The retention of Noyes to command the battalion of the Second Cavalry was proof positive that the charge of neglect of duty during the Powder River was nothing more than a "good-natured farce."

Five companies of infantry accompanied the expedition. They were under the command of one of Crook's West Point classmates, Major Alexander Chambers. The infantry units included three companies of the Ninth and two of the Fourth Infantry. Captain Azor H. Nickerson and Lieutenant Bourke were appointed aides-de-camp. Captain George M. Randall was made Chief of Scouts, an empty title, since no scouts had been enlisted. Other staff and their positions were: Captain William Stanton as Chief Engineer Officer, Captain John V. Furey as Chief Quartermaster, Lieutenant John W. Bubb as Commissary of Subsistence, and Assistant Surgeon Albert Hartsuff as Medical Director.[10]

Officers of the individual companies:

Third Cavalry
Company A - Lt. Charles Morton
Company B - Captain Charles Meinhold; Lt. James F. Simpson
Company C - Captain Frederick Van Vliet; Lt. Adolphus H. Von Leuttwitz
Company D - Captain Guy V. Henry; Lt. William W. Robinson, Jr.
Company E - Captain Alexander Sutorius
Company F - Lt. Bainbridge Reynolds

Company G - Lt. Emmet Crawford
Company I - Captain William H. Andrews; Lt. James E.H. Foster; Lt. Albert D. King
Company L - Captain Peter D. Vroom; Lt. George F. Chase
Company M - Captain Anson Mills; Lt. Augustus C. Paul; Lt. Frederick Schwatka
Second Cavalry
Company A - Captain Thomas B. Dewees; Lt. Daniel C. Pearson
Company B - Lt. William C. Rawolle
Company D - Lt. Samuel M. Swigert; Lt. Henry D. Huntington
Company E - Captain Elijah R. Wells; Lt. Frederick W. Sibley
Company I - Captain Henry E. Noyes; Lt. Fred W. Kingsbury
Ninth Infantry
Company C - Captain Samuel Munson; Lt. Thaddeus Capron
Company G - Captain Thomas B. Burrowes; Lt. W.L. Carpenter
Company H - Captain Andrew S. Burt; Lt. Edgar B. Robertson
Fourth Infantry
Company D - Captain Avery B. Cain; Lt. Henry Seton
Company F - Captain Gerhard Luhn
Additional Headquarters Staff and Personnel
Assistant Surgeons - Julius H. Patzki; Charles R. Stevens; Junius L. Powell
Chief of Pack Train - Thomas Moore
Chief of Wagon Train - Charles Russell
Guides - Frank Grouard, Louis Richaud, Baptiste Pourrier (Big Bat)

A demi-company of newspaper reporters accompanied the column to chronicle the events. Representing the press corps were John F. Finerty, the "Irish pencil pusher" of the *Chicago Times;* Thomas B. MacMillian, *Chicago Inter-Ocean;* Reuben H. Davenport, *New York Herald;* Robert A. Strahorn, reporting under the nom-de-plume "Alter Ego" for the Denver *Rocky Mountain News;* and Joseph Wasson of the *San Francisco Alta California.*

Several officers maintained diaries which have proven beneficial in relating the history of the campaign. Chief diarist was John Bourke. Bourke's account of the summer campaign later evolved into one of the most important and widely quoted books of the expedition, *On the Border With Crook*.[11] The official itinerist, Captain William Stanton, and infantry officers Captain Gerhard L. Luhn and Lieutenant Thaddeus H. Capron also preserved important diaries and letters. Cavalry lieutenant James Foster produced a journal later used by the *Chicago Tribune*. Foster also supplied sketches to *Harper's Weekly*.[12]

At noon on May 29, 1876, the command departed from Fetterman. Stretching out four miles, the column took on the appearance of a thin black ribbon as it snaked its way northward across the Wyoming prairie. Its path was identical to that of the March expedition up the Bozeman Trail. Dust from the sun-baked trail soon hovered above the men in a thick cloud before settling back onto the men and animals, choking everyone.

Besides the 900 men of the command, there were 103 wagons, each pulled by a six-mule team.

The column was military in look although individuality of dress and personal comfort were prime considerations on long campaigns. Rigid military dress codes found at garrisons were normally relaxed on extended marches. Crook was dressed in an old hunting jacket, slouch felt hat, and soldier's boots, his beard braided and taped.[13] Later the general would add an enlisted man's overcoat to his simple but picturesque wardrobe.[14] Crook's officers were only a trifle better dressed.

For the most part, the uniform and equipment of the enlisted men were standard issue. Each trooper wore either a leftover Civil War, four-button drab blue blouse or one of the newer-model, five-button blouses. Made of loose fitting wool, each tunic was fastened by brass eagle buttons. Sky-blue baggy woolen trousers worn by cavalrymen were reinforced in the seat with strips of canvas or cloth, and were held up by suspenders. Infantrymen wore leather bootees or Jefferson boots, dyed black, the soles fastened with brass screws. Cavalrymen wore the Model 1872 boots, which came up about mid-way to the calf.

Headgear showed little standardization. Some soldiers wore the prescribed black felt hat with its floppy broad brim, while others preferred civilian pattern hats. Sturdy straw hats seemed to have been very popular among the men. Others opted to wear the 1872 kepi with its short leather visor. Normally the kepi was worn in garrison.

Armament for the cavalry consisted of the Model 1873 Springfield "trapdoor" carbine, caliber .45, and a sidearm, the Model 1873 Colt, single action revolver, .45 caliber. The Springfield rifle, long barrel cousin to the cavalry carbine, was standard issue to the infantry. In accuracy and range the rifle was superior to the carbine. The rifle was effective up to 1,000 yards, the carbine to about 600 yards. Ammunition was carried on canvas or leather waistbelts affixed with canvas or leather loops, rather than in regulation pouches. The waistbelts had a decided advantage over the pouches in that they allowed for even weight distribution of the heavy metallic cartridges.

Cavalrymen had an advantage over their infantry counterparts in that extra gear could be tied to the saddles or carried in saddle bags. Both were issued haversacks in which rations, plates, and utensils were kept. A canteen, another holdover from Civil War days, held about a pint of water. Infantrymen carried a blanket and rubber poncho bedroll. It was rolled up and the ends tied, then suspended from the right shoulder.[15]

But Crook's thoughts were not dwelling on the dress of the men. He was anxious to acquire scouts, the eyes and ears of the army. He had found no support at the agencies. As he rode up the trail, his mind undoubtedly turned toward the anticipated arrival of Crows and Shoshones, both tribes traditional enemies of the Sioux. So keen was he on soliciting their aid that he had ordered a battalion forward, May 28, to locate them.

This important task was assigned to Company C under Cap-

tain Van Vliet and Company G under the command of Lieutenant Emmet Crawford. Outfitted with eight day's rations, they
were dispatched ahead to Fort Reno, where it was hoped they
would locate the allies.[16]   The first day's march took the command as far as Sage Creek, about 12 miles from Fetterman. The
day had been uneventful, and the evening passed in quiet repose.
That evening Captain Gerhard Luhn wrote home to his wife,
stationed at Fort Laramie, "General Crook dined with us and
praised your rye bread very highly."[17]

On the 30th, Crook evidenced growing concern about the
allies and, to a lesser degree, sought information on Sioux activities in the region. To this end two more companies, Captain
Meinhold's and Vroom's, were dispatched westward from Sage
Creek to reconnoiter. Taking four day's rations, the detachment
left to rejoin the column at old Fort Reno.[18]

The main force proceeded northwest, reaching the South
Cheyenne River after a march of 20 miles. It wasn't much of a
river, Bourke noted in his diary, just "a shriveled stream of
muddy and alkaline water standing in pools."[19]

Moderate temperatures, which had been the bench mark of
the first two days were supplanted on the 31st by a cold brace of
winds out of the north. The monotonous bleak terrain was little
company for the soldiers, who donned overcoats to keep warm.[20]
Twenty miles were made, and camp pitched on the North Fork
of Wind River. Finerty labeled the creek "a very poor apology
for a stream."[21] During the evening the first casualty of the
campaign was reported. A messenger arrived from Meinhold's
command with news of an accident. A trooper in Meinhold's
company had accidentally shot himself. Dr. Hartsuff and an
ambulance wagon was sent to bring in the injured soldier.[22] The
unfortunate trooper turned out to be Private Francis Tierney.
Brought back to camp, Tierney was found to be in great agony.
Little could be done for him except to make him comfortable,
the wound proving mortal. Details of the accident indicated that

Tierney had carelessly thrown his revolver to the ground to chop firewood for the evening meal. The gun discharged, with the bullet striking the trooper in the leg and ultimately coming to rest in the left kidney.[23]

The troops awakened on the first of June to a winter-like snowstorm. Reporter Finerty quipped that he thought the command had inadvertently reached Alaska. Despite the pelting snow driven by fierce winds, the imperturable Crook pushed on. The column was up and on the road by five o'clock. Later in the campaign, Crook modified marching orders by putting the infantry under way at six o'clock, with the cavalry following at seven-thirty. The extra time for the cavalry was allotted out of consideration, to rest them before the more arduous task expected to lie ahead.[24]

By noon the storm had subsided, giving way to clearing skies and rising temperatures. After a march of 20 miles, they made camp on the Dry Fork of Powder River. Captain Meinhold rejoined the command after discovering no new road to Fort Reno or any signs of Indians, friendly or otherwise.[25]

June 2 broke raw and cold. The Big Horn and Yellowstone Expedition continued to set a northwest course. Vestiges of the Big Horn Mountains with their snow-capped peaks towered on the far distant horizon. To the east the square-shaped plateau of Pumpkin Buttes could be easily discerned, while, still further to the east, the dark blotches outlining the Black Hills could be seen with the aid of binoculars. Behind the men, growing dimmer with each passing mile, lay Laramie Peak.

Enroute between Dry Fork and Fort Reno, the men discovered evidence in the form of rifle pits that miners had recently passed by. A wooden board with a message dated May 27, 1876, declared that Captain St. John's party of miners was headed for the Black Hills mining district of Whitewood.[26]

Approaching Fort Reno, situated on the left bank of the Powder River, the ever popular Captain Anson Mills became involved in an amusing incident with the notorious woman "Calamity Jane." The embarrassed captain later recounted his misfortune:

> In organizing the wagon train at Fort Fetterman the wagon-master had unintentionally employed a female teamster, but she was not discovered until we neared Fort Reno, when she was suddenly arrested, and placed in improvised female attire under guard. I knew nothing of this, but being the senior Captain of Cavalry, having served as a Captain for sixteen years, and being an inquisitive turn of mind, I had become somewhat notorious (for better or worse).
>
> The day she was discovered and placed under guard, unconscious of the fact, I was going through the wagon-master's outfit when she sprang up, calling "there is Colonel Mills, he knows me" when everybody began to laugh, much to my astonishment and chagrin, being married.
>
> It was not many hours until every man in the camp knew of the professed familiarity of "Calamity Jane". I, of course, denied any knowledge of her or her calling, but no one believed me then, and I doubt very much whether they all do yet.
>
> We carried her along until a force was organized to carry our helpless back, with which she was sent, but she afterwards turned out to be a national character, and was a woman of no mean ability and force even from the standard of men. I learned later that she had been a resident of North Platte, and that she knew many of my soldiers, some of whom had probably betrayed her. Later she had employed herself as a cook for my next-door neighbor, Lieutenant Johnson, and had seen me often in his house, I presume.[27]

Crook's thoughts on the matter were not recorded. A fretting Crook was more concerned with his overdue scouts. He had hoped they would be at Reno. Instead he met Van Vliet's command, who informed him they they had not seen any sign of the allies. Extremely anxious to have guides, he summoned three of his white scouts, Frank Grouard, Louis Richaud, and Baptiste

Pourrier "Big Bat," to his tent. They were instructed to travel posthaste to the Crow Agency, then located on the Stillwater near Livingston, Montana. Crook admonished the trio to use whatever means necessary to enlist the services of the Crows.[28] In conferring with the three men, he was advised their mission might consume several weeks. It was suggested to the general that the main command push on to the Goose Creek forks near present-day Sheridan. Goose Creek offered the advantage of ample water and fresh grazing pasture for the animals. Using a cloak of darkness for a screen, the intrepid scouts bade farewell to their comrades and started off on their dangerous journey. Crow Agency lay 300 miles away and would angle through country thought to be teeming with Sioux and Cheyenne.[29]

Since their arrival at Reno, the men had been in an upbeat mood. Emotions were fueled by the dilapidated ruins of the post, which reflected past turmoil with refractory Indians. Vestiges of human occupation in the form of iron debris littered the ground. To the sharp wit of Finerty, the scene was a Chicago junk dealer's dream come true. The enduring sight confronting most of the soldiers was the pitiful ruins of the post cemetery. What had once served as permanent markers honoring the final resting places of soldiers killed a decade ago in the line of duty, now lay in utter ruin. Images of desecrated graves were a burning reminder for many of the men, eager to seek out the perpetrators and even the score.[30]

Leaving Reno behind, the command moved forward on the 3rd. The day would be long. The next watering hole lay 30 miles away and would necessitate a grueling march. As usual, Crook and his staff assumed the lead, followed by his infantry and cavalry. The morning's trek was pleasant. A thin film of white frost sparkled in the sunlight. The frost was welcomed relief, for it helped reduce the billowing clouds of choking dust continually kicked up. Although the scenery was bland, some soldiers could not help but notice that spring had emerged on the Northern

Plains. Everywhere the prairie was carpeted with tender young shoots of verdant grass.[31]

Around noon several purported Indian signal fires were observed. Companies of cavalry were dispatched to investigate but returned having found nothing. That evening bivouac was made on Crazy Woman Creek. Fed by the icy waters of the Big Horn Mountains, the stream ran swift and cold. A decade before, Crazy Woman Creek had been the site of bitterly contested battles between Sioux and the U.S. Army. As a precautionary measure, pickets were strengthened to patrol the camp and guard against sudden surprises.[32]

June 4 was a shorter march, about 20 miles. Camp was made on the bank of Clear Creek. Ninth infantrymen exploring the area near camp discovered an Indian burial scaffold. Not needing any words of encouragement, the soldiers quickly vandalized the corpse on its bier for its contents. The wooden support poles were highly coveted. They were taken back to camp and chopped up for kindling, which was used to cook the evening meal. Of this incident the talented Finerty wrote: "Thus the relationship of all men to each other in point of savagery was established. The Sioux defaced the white graves at Reno. The whites converted the Sioux pedestal into kindling-wood. It was all the same to the dead on both sides."[33]

While the men were camped on Clear Fork, two miners sauntered into the bivouac. They explained they were part of a mining party coming out of the Black Hills, bound for the Big Horns. Their camp, they said, was a day behind. Although no one from Crook down to the lowliest private could at the time forsee it, the value of the miners would be proven at the Rosebud.[34]

On the 5th of June, Crook's command passed Lake De Smet and halted for the evening at the site of Fort Phil Kearny. Total distance traveled was 16 miles. Camp was pitched along Big Piney, east of the fort.[35] Like Reno, old Fort Phil Kearny stirred the emotions of the men. Lt. Capron writing to his wife, Cynthia recounted his impression of the fort:

> . . . We saw the remains of Fort Phil Kearney [*sic*], of which very little was left. A portion of the charred stockade and a few posts at the corner of an old brick yard, with a huge pile of broken brick; the sweeps and boxes for mixing the clay; and last the cemetery, which contains all that remains of those who met their fate at the Fetterman massacre. They lie buried in one large grave — eighty-one! The vandals had broken down the monument of brick that was erected to mark their resting place, but the immense grave had not been disturbed. The place was one of the worst that could have been selected for a military post, as it was almost surrounded by high hills, from which the Indians could fire into the post.[36]

The route on the 6th passed over Lodge Trail Ridge. The course was the same traversed by the ill-fated Fetterman ten years before. Large boulders marked the site where Fetterman and Brown were reported to have fallen.[37] As the column descended Fetterman's Ridge, many soldiers' thoughts turned from the Fetterman debacle to visions of trout fishing. Goose Creek was only a dozen miles away. In fact Captain Luhn noted in his diary, "Several officers carried their fishing poles thinking they would strike Goose Creek in a few hours from camp."[38] Unfortunately for the fishermen of the outfit, there would be no fishing this day. By a quirk of fate or a case of just plain bad luck in navigation, the command took the wrong route after leaving Fetterman Ridge. The army turned north, following the sinuous course of Prairie Dog Creek, and away from the forks of the Goose Creek.

Oblivious to his mistake, Crook trudged onward for 18 miles, not realizing the contretemps until it was too late. An afternoon cloudburst added to their woes. The men settled down to a dull camp along Prairie Dog amid a pelting rain.[39] Things could hardly deteriorate any more for Crook, or could they? Unbeknownst to Crook and his men, a small party of Cheyennes including Wooden Leg, out on a hunting foray, accidentally stumbled onto the rainy encampment. Concealing themselves from view, they followed the bluecoats for a day before returning to their main village, situated on the Rosebud.[40]

Not all the soldiers were as poor pathfinders as Crook. That morning Captain Noyes, with a party of ten men, had marched out in advance to locate a suitable camping spot on Goose Creek and to stake out squatter's rights to prime fishing holes. Crook's failure to show up on schedule suggested to Noyes that something must have gone amiss. Noyes and his men backtracked in search of the wayward expedition.[41] They picked up the trail on the Prairie Dog and began to follow it. Darkness and the rainstorm overtook Noyes before he could contact the column. Noyes opted to camp apart from the command lest some nervous picket begin firing into his small detachment. His arrival next morning brought relief to a concerned Crook.[42]

An inexplicable development occurred the morning of June 7. Crook was fully cognizant, as were his officers, that the column was headed in the wrong direction. To continue north down Prairie Dog would only take them further away from Goose Creek. Yet Crook elected to proceed down the creek. His reasoning for continuing in the wrong direction was never explained. A man of few words, he said nothing. Orders were given to move out.

Captain Andrews' company assumed the lead, acting as pioneers for the rest of the column.[43]

The terrain was rugged. Animals experienced agonizing pains, and wagons were put to severe tests in attempting to make their way over broken ground cut up by deep ravines and gullies. After an exhausting journey of 17 miles they reached the mouth of the creek on Tongue River near the present Wyoming-Montana border. Camp was made beneath steep bluffs commanding the north bank of the Tongue.

The day ended with solemnity. The unfortunate trooper wounded on Meinhold's scout, Private Andrew Tierney, died in camp.[44] A military funeral was ordered with all the dignity and honor befitting the occasion. Bourke, impressed by the event recorded:

> Besides the escort prescribed by the regulations, the funeral cortege was swollen by additions from all the companies of the expedition, the pack-train, wagoners, officers, and others, reaching an aggregate of over six hundred. Colonel Guy V. Henry, Third Cavalry, read in a very telling manner at the burial service from the "Book of Common Prayer," the cavalry trumpets sounded "taps," a handful of earth was thrown down upon the remains, the grave was rapidly filled up, and the companies at quick step returned to their tents. There was no labored panegyric delivered over the body of Tiernan [*sic*], but the kind reminiscences of his comrades were equivalent to an eulogy of which an archbishop might have been proud.[45]

A large flat rock requiring ten men to move was placed over his grave. Tierney's name was inscribed in the rock.[46]

General Crook, an avid enthusiast in natural history, meandered off to search for specimens of fauna.[47] Ignorant to Crook, other species were wandering toward his camp. About midnight, voices in an unknown Indian dialect were discerned on the bluff across the river. Courier Ben Arnold was dispatched to see if he could open up communications. Arnold had no luck in distinguishing the voices or the dialect. Finally, Arnold responded in the Siouxan tongue. With that, the mystery guests vanished into the black night. Crook was justifiably angered over Arnold's slip of the tongue, for he correctly surmised, as it turned out later, that the voices were those of his expected Crow scouts.[48]

That pervasive mill known as rumor became rampant. Everyone had their own idea on the subject. Reuben Davenport, reporter for the *New York Herald,* was quick to draw his own conclusion. Writing for the *Herald,* June 16, 1876, he claimed the voices announced the impending doom for the command if not removed from the area within two days.[49]

The 8th was marked for a day of rest, the men and animals enjoying a well-deserved respite from the campaign's rigors. Some of the men tried their hand at fishing, but found the recent rains had thoroughly muddied the Tongue. Trout fishing was poor, but leave it to a soldier to find an ersatz. Improvised seines were fashioned, and in that manner a haul of shad was made.[50]

A cavalry patrol investigating the bluffs where the phantom voices were heard the night before, found fresh tracks belonging to five riders. One pony was discovered grazing, but otherwise nothing else was found. During the day, 65 miners joined the camp. But the biggest event of the day was the arrival of two couriers. They brought the first news of the outside world since leaving Fort Fetterman ten days ago. Dispatches from Sheridan revealed encouraging information! 120 Shoshones were on their way to join the column and would arrive in a few days. Also, the Fifth Cavaly had embarked from Kansas to bolster Crook's rear. The dispatches further disclosed what Crook already suspected — warriors from the Red Cloud Agency had left the reservation. One other bit of discouraging information was noted. The telegraph wires connecting Crow Agency had been severed, indicating the Crows had not received the call to arms against their foes.[51]

Crook waited out the 9th in camp, perhaps expecting the scouts to return. To break the boredom which now engulfed the camp, some of the more enterprising men amused themselves by arranging horse races. Captain Burt's fine blooded mount won two races. At approximately 6:30 P.M. when Burt was cooling off his horse, the stillness was breached by a fusillade from the bluffs beyond the camp. Whining bullets splintered the air, striking the ground and ventilating the camp tents arranged neatly in order. Because the camp was situated in the bottom the area was difficult to defend. Officers and noncommissioned staffs barked out commands. Companies C, G, and H, Ninth Infantry, in column of fours, marched in natty order to support the pickets on the hills. Company C led the advance, flanked on the right by Company H and on the left and rear by Company G.[52] The infantry crossed the river and started up the bluffs. The Indians did not wait to see the infantry's intentions. They had too much respect to tangle with the long-range weapons of the foot soldiers. Quickly they left the infantry in their dust and moved upstream. Lieutenant Capron fondly recalled that "the zipping of the bullets reminded me of days gone by."[53]

Meanwhile, upriver, a staff officer reached the nervous Captain Mills with instructions to mount his men, cross the river, and clear the bluffs of Indians.[54] In scarcely less time than it took to deliver the edict, Mills had his battalion of four companies wading over the Tongue. To cover Mills and offer some support, a company from the Second Cavalry was detailed to move beyond Mills' left and take up a protective position among the cottonwood trees lining the Tongue.

Dismounting on the opposite bank, Mills had one horse holder for every eight troopers. The remainder of the cavalrymen began scaling the precipitous bluffs. Mills' "rock climbers" from left to right consisted of companies A, M, E, and I. Topping the bluff, they discovered the assailants had scurried to another ridge about 1000 yards away. Long-range shots were exchanged, but did no one any harm. Mills advanced with his line of skirmishers. The Indians broke and ran to the next ridge. After realizing the futility in bringing his adversary to battle, Mills ordered a halt. The sound of firing to Mills' rear indicated more trouble back at camp. Ordering an "About Face", Mills returned to camp and found it buzzing. A party of warriors had circled behind the camp in an endeavor to drive off some of the livestock. The pickets of the Second Cavalry saw their motives and easily drove them back.[55]

The entire affair lasted nearly one hour.[56] Actually, the raid served as an antidote to break the monotony of the campaign. The attack produced an exhilarating mood among the men. Indeed, it bolstered their morale and elevated their confidence, that they could easily handle anything the Indians threw at them.

Casualties were minimal: two soldiers slightly wounded by spent bullets, three horses and a mule killed, recorded reporter Davenport.[57] Sergeant Warfield, Company F, Third Cavalry received a slight wound in the right arm, while Private Emil Renner, Company D, Second Cavalry, had a flesh wound in the left thigh.[58] Davenport, who rode with Mills, claimed two Indians were wounded, although no bodies were recovered.[59]

Of the horses killed, the beautiful white mount of Captain Burt was among them. A bullet had broken its leg, and the animal had to be destroyed.[60] Another casualty was the stovepipe of Mills' Sibley stove. Bullets had perforated the flue, causing it to resemble a piece of Swiss cheese.

Estimates to the number of Indians in the attack produced wide ranging figures. Some said at least 900, while at the other end of the spectrum, 50 was surmised. In fact, it was only a few Cheyennes under Little Hawk. They had returned to the area following Wooden Leg's report that soldiers were coming. Little Hawk's band sought out the bluecoats in hopes of stealing a few horses. Their plans were thwarted because at the time of their attack the horses were picketed for grooming.[61]

In the evening additional guards were positioned as a precautionary measure. Company B, Second Cavalry was sent across the river and posted on the high bluffs.[62] The camp settled down to its usual routine. A steady cold rain began falling during the night.

CHAPTER IV
"Trout Fishing After All"

Crook remained one more day on the Tongue before breaking camp and moving to where he was supposed to have gone in the first place — the forks of Goose Creek. Simultaneously, he sent a dispatch to Sheridan with information about the skirmish on the 9th. Dated the 11th, the message revealed something of Crook's concerns over the absence of his scouts. Furthermore, Crook felt the Indian attack was made to conceal the movement of the Indian village, which Crook surmised was located on the Little Rosebud or Tongue River.[1]

The command retraced its route up Prairie Dog Creek for 11 miles before turning west. After a march of seven miles, the column reached Goose Creek. Owing to an afternoon hailstorm, the trip was rendered all the more difficult.

Camp on Goose Creek was delightful. Luxuriant growths of grasses carpeted the valley. There was a plentiful supply of wood and clear swift water, the latter fed by snow melts in the Big Horns. Until the arrival of the scouts, there was little to do except fish and hunt. Fisherman Luhn delighted in writing to his wife that he would "have some trout fishing after all."[2]

Some of the officers continued to amuse themselves by organizing impromptu horse races staking sides of venison or a can of corn as the purse. The camp was made even more delightful by rising temperatures. It also brought out large numbers of rattlesnakes. Lieutenant Lemly killed one such creature that had crawled inside his blanket.[3] Despite the occasional encounters with rattlesnakes, the entire mood of the camp was one of a summer's picnic.

But Crook's temperament was one of continual concern for his scouts. On June 13, 1876, he ordered Lieutenant Samuel Swigert with a detail of men to old Fort Phil Kearny to see if he could locate the overdue Shoshones. Swigert returned in the evening empty-handed.[4] Capron recorded in his diary, "the General is quite weary and nervous, and it is thought that he is feeling very anxious about the safety of the guides that were sent out from [Fort] Reno."[5]

Crook's anxiety turned to relief on the 14th. Scouts Frank Grouard and Louis Richaud arrived to a cheering throng of soldiers and teamsters. Accompanying them was one impressive looking, if somewhat aged, Crow Indian. Crook interrogated his scouts. He was delighted to learn that in their wake, about ten miles behind, "Big Bat" Pourrier was holding about 175 Crows. The Crow delegation Crook learned, was a bit tentative about entering the soldier's camp. A battery of questions soon discovered the problem.

It had been a Crow scouting party of 15 led by "Big Bat" which had stumbled onto Crook's pickets on the Tongue, June 7. When Ben Arnold answered their call in the Sioux tongue they were afraid they had blundered into a Sioux village. To compound the problem they returned later, only to discover evidence that the soldiers had vanished, giving rise to the idea that Crook had retreated. The Crows were reluctant to support the soldiers in the face of this show of all talk and no action. Only the prodding of the scouts prevented the total disbandment of the Crows.

Crook reaffirmed the Crow Chief of the Army's intentions to fight the Crow's enemies. In another diplomatic manipulation, Crook ordered Captain Andrew S. Burt to accompany the Crow party into camp. The selection of Andy Burt for the escort mission was indeed wise, for Burt personally knew many of the Crows, having once been stationed at Fort C.F. Smith.[6]

Crook learned from his Crow informant that when Gibbon had been camped opposite the mouth of the Big Horn River, the Sioux had been bold and successful in fully crossing the Yellowstone and raiding the Crow pony herd. The old Crow disclosed that presently Gibbon's force was opposite the mouth of the Rosebud. He further revealed that the Sioux were on the south side of the Yellowstone, believed to be somewhere on the Tongue, between the mouth of Otter Creek and the Yellowstone River.[7]

In retrospect, the intelligence gathered at this meeting was vague at best. It was certainly outdated. The theft of the Crow horses had occurred on May 3.[8] And what of Gibbon's camp opposite the mouth of Rosebud Creek? Did this mean the Sioux were on the Rosebud instead of the Tongue as the Crow suggested? Frank Grouard did not think the Sioux were on the Tongue. He told the General, "from all signs I had seen I supposed they were on the Rosebud..."[9]

As Crook pondered his next move in the cat and mouse game, an uproar could be heard throughout the camp. The contingent of Crows were seen approaching, led by their chiefs, Old Crow, Medicine Crow, and Good Heart.[10] The observant Bourke noted their arrival:

Our newly-arrived allies bivouacked in our midst, sending their herd of ponies out to graze alongside of our own horses. The entire band numbered one hundred and seventy-six, as near as we could ascertain; each had two ponies. The first thing they did was to erect the war lodges of saplings, covered over with blankets or pieces of canvas; fires were next built, and a feast prepared of the supplies of coffee, sugar, and hardtack dealt out by the commissary; these are the prime luxuries of an Indian's life. A curious crowd of lookers-on — officers, soldiers, teamsters, and packers — congregated around the little squads of Crows, watching with eager attention their every movement. The Indians seemed proud of the distinguished position they occupied in popular estimation and were soon on terms of easy familiarity with the soldiers, some of whom could talk a sentence or two of Crow, and others were expert to a slight extent in the sign language.[11]

No sooner had the fanfare welcoming the Crows subsided, when the hubbub was renewed again. From the south the Shoshones were approaching. At the head of the column rode ex-Confederate Tom Cosgrove.[12] Cheering soldiers greeted their entrance. Again, the keen eyes and finely tuned pen of Bourke captured the moment:

> . . . The Shoshones or Snakes, who, to the number of eight-six galloped rapidly up to headquarters and came left front into line in splendid style. No trained warriors of civilized armies ever executed the movement more prettily. Exclamations of wonder and praise greeted the barbaric array of these fierce warriors, warmly welcomed by their former enemies but at present strong friends — the Crows. General Crook moved out to review their line of battle, resplendent in all the fantastic adornment of feathers, beads, brass buttons, bells, scarlet cloth, and flashing lances. The Shoshones were not slow to perceive the favorable impression made, and when the order came for them to file off by the right moved with the precision of clockwork and the pride of veterans.[13]

Of the two groups, Bourke deemed the Shoshones the better disciplined. In armament, the Shoshones were likewise better armed, carrying .45 caliber Springfields, while most of the Crows possessed .50 caliber rifles.[14]

Following "retreat", Crook summoned his battalion commanders to his headquarter's tent. Simple, but terse instructions, were delivered by Crook. He informed the assemblage gathered that they were to leave the wagons behind. Every man, officer and enlistee was to carry four days rations of hardtack, bacon, and coffee. One hundred rounds of ammunition was to be carried either in belts or pouches. Tentage would be left behind and the men instructed to bring along one blanket each. All able-bodied infantrymen would be outfitted with a mule for riding. Assuming they located and successfully attacked a village, all food provisions captured would be preserved for later consumption or be used, should the command continue downstream to unite or meet with Gibbon and Terry.[15] The tone and message of Crook's comments were taken to heart. Reporter Finerty revealed "Crook was bristling for a fight,"[16] to which Bourke added, "The General meant business."[17]

The camp was a beehive of activity on June 15. Quartermaster Captain John V. Furey took charge of the base camp. He and any disabled soldiers would remain behind to superintend the camp. In all, Furey had about 100 men at his disposal, including some teamsters and packers. The day also marked orientation day for the infantrymen. One hundred and seventy-five foot soldiers were marched out to a grassy meadow to receive a rudimentary lesson in mule riding. A delightfully large throng of curious cavalrymen congregated, anticipating a show. They were not to be disappointed. What followed could unofficially serve as Sheridan's first rodeo. Head scout Frank Grouard fondly recalled: "I never saw so much fun in all my life. The valley, for a mile in every direction, was filled with bucking mules, frightened infantrymen, broken saddles and applauding spectators."[18] Even the Indian allies got caught up in the commotion. They jumped on the mules to show the wild-eyed infantrymen how easy the mules could be mastered. Needless to say, the "Walk a Heaps" were not amused with the circus at their expense.

By afternoon, the individual companies had completed their last minute details in preparation for the march next morning. One other item needed attending. Private William Nelson of Company L, Third Cavalry had died on the evening before. He was administered last rites and laid to rest at sunset on the 15th.[19]

Crook's strike force was impressive: 1000 officers and enlisted men, 260 Indian scouts, and 85 miners and packers, a total force exceeding 1300. The breakdown of men by battalions and departments was as follows:[20]

Troop Strength

Second Cavalry, battalion of Capt. Henry Noyes 269
Third Cavalry, battalion of Capt. Anson Mills 207
Third Cavalry, battalion of Lt. Col. William Royall.......... 327
Infantry, battalion of Major Alexander Chambers 175
Crow Scouts 176
Shoshones Scouts 86
Packers 20
Montana Miners 65

Total Force   1325

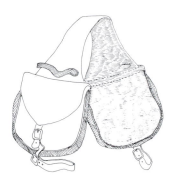

CHAPTER V

March to the Rosebud

The largest expeditionary command on the Northern Plains since the 1865 campaign of scrappy pugilist, General Patrick E. Connor's, broke camp at 5 A.M. June 16, 1876.[1] Morale was high, confidence supreme. As usual, Crook rode in the van, accompanied by his staff and scouts. Principal leaders of the Crows included Old Crow, Medicine Crow, and Good Heart. The Shoshones were divided into two groups commanded by Tom Cosgrove and Louissant.[2] The cavalcade marched north following the current route of U.S. Highway 87. Approaching the Tongue River, the column skirted the left bank in order to avoid broken terrain.[3] Gradually the route swung northwest, traversing the divide, separating the watersheds of Tongue and Rosebud Valley. Reporters remarked on the captivating beauty of the country. The region was covered with an emerald green carpet of grasses. About noon, a halt was ordered on the divide of Spring Creek, while scouts went in search of Sioux. During the interlude, soldiers settled down to a prolong wait, some of the men taking the opportunity to boil coffee.[4] What caught the eyes of the scouts was a large buffalo herd grazing in the distance. Unbeknownst to them, that same herd of bison was being investigated by a small band of Cheyennes. Under Little Hawk, a party of warriors had left the main Indian encampment, then located on Reno Creek about thirty miles to the north, to hunt.

They had been joined by another Cheyenne group from Magpie Eagle's camp located on Trail Creek, a tributary of the Rosebud.[5] By accident, the two parties had blundered onto the identical herd.[6] Frank Grouard and Plenty Coups of the Crows exchanged visual insults before the Cheyennes scattered. Returning to Crook, the scouts reported the incident to him. Grouard informed the General that the Indians were seen heading toward the Rosebud. This information gives rise to the theory that the village was located somewhere on the Rosebud.[7] However, the great encampment was not on the Rosebud. Instead, it was situated on Reno Creek, a branch of the Little Bighorn, about 30 miles to the northwest.

The Cheyennes from Magpie Eagle's band returned to their encampment to warn their compatriots of the nearby soldiers. Meanwhile, Little Hawk's group scurried to the main village and broke the news that soldiers were on the upper Rosebud. Aroused by the presence and movements of bluecoats to the south, the Indians began to prepare to meet their foes in combat. The warriors donned their finest habiliments and tied up their ponies' tails for war. Singely, in pairs, in groups, and by bands, the Indians on the night of June 16, began to ride southward to contest the approaching soldiers. Exactly how many Indians participated in the upcoming battle is a matter of conflicting reports and estimates. Guesses range from a low of 750 upwards to 2000 or more.[8] Whatever the real number, there were more than enough warriors to fully frustrate Crook the next day.[9]

But for now, Crook was annoyed with another matter — his scouts. Throughout the day his Indian auxillaries had comported themselves as if they were on a glorified picnic. Countless buffalo were seen and killed by the scouts. If Crook expected to surprise the Sioux this was certain to blunt any chance. Inwardly, he raged over the incident, but outwardly, his demeanor was complete reticent. He so valued the scouts on campaign that he dare not chastize them too much, less he run the risk of having them abandon him. So he said nothing.[10]

Satisfied the Indians were headed for their camp on the Rosebud, Crook could at least take comfort that he was going in the right direction. The day's march of 35 miles ended at 7:20 P.M. Camp was pitched at the head of south fork of Rosebud Creek. First into camp was the cavalry. They formed a square surrounding a small lake, leaving one side of the rectangle open for the infantrymen. The cavalry, still remembering the entertainment provided by the foot soldiers the day before, began to mass at the open side of the square, hoping for another chance to good-naturedly jab at their companions. The mule-riding infantry came up in good order and took their designated places in line. At the command "halt," the mules seemingly on cue, commenced in unison a chorus of brays, filling the camp with laughter. Major Chambers, however, was not at all humored by the outcry. Uttering a string of blue oaths, Chambers slammed his sword to the ground and left the command to fend for itself.[11]

If Crook was dissatisfied with the intelligence gathering of his scouts during the day, he had more to be chagrined with during the evening. Painfully aware that the Sioux were nearby, he urged his scouts to go out during the night. Most of them declined, fearing the presence of Sioux.[12] One small party did venture forth. They discovered an abandoned campfire and a blanket of India-rubber.[13]

The reluctance on the part of Crook's scouts to conduct important reconnaissance created graver problems the next day. While Crook's scouts sat idling in camp the Indians were engaged in nocturnal activities. Cheyennes under Young Two Moon, Two Moon, and Spotted Wolf approached the Rosebud via Trail Creek. Sioux under the able guidance of Crazy Horse traveled up the south fork of Reno Creek and down Corral Creek to intersect the Rosebud. Other warriors converged on the upper reaches of Rosebud by crossing Sioux Pass.[14] Sitting Bull would go, but he was so weakened from his sun dance ordeal that he could do nothing more than be a spectator, offering words of encouragement.

All the Indians, Sioux and Cheyenne, shared two common goals: drive the hated bluecoats from their lands, and gain as many war honors as possible.

That night, a light rain descended upon Crook's camp, bringing a soothing relief from the day's heat.[15] Perhaps as a premonition, Bourke wrote in his diary, 'We are now right in among the hostiles and may strike or be struck at any hour.''[16] Tomorrow would make Bourke a prophet. The soldiers slept. The next day, some would find eternal sleep.

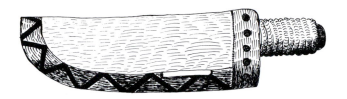

CHAPTER VI

"They are Shooting Buffaloes Over There"

The first gray streaks of dawn appeared on the Montana horizon at 3 A.M. Already there was stirring in the camp. Scouts fumbled about in dim light. The singing and festivities that had been their hallmark on the 16th now yielded to icy silence. The solitude was mute testimony to wholesome respect they accorded the Sioux. Every scout knew full well they were in the heart of Sioux domain. The soldiers' countenances were entirely different. The men sipped their coffee, joked and chatted with each other, or tried to take quick catnaps prior to the command's scheduled 6 A.M. departure.

As was the custom with Crook, the infantry was the first on the road, followed by the cavalry, and then the packers and miners. Little time had elapsed before the swifter moving horsemen had overtaken the infantry and assumed the advance. The column plodded northward down the south fork of Rosebud Creek. The Rosebud itself was a sluggish little stream, not over twenty yards wide in anyplace, and less than ten yards in most places. Thickets of wild roses in blossom covered parts of the creek bank, giving the stream its name. Beyond the banks bordering the creek, the valley was a mixture of brilliant colors. A sea of blue wildflowers punctuated the green landscape.

Marching parallel on opposite sides of the Rosebud, the serpentine-like army had covered less than three miles when the

north fork of the Rosebud came in on the left. Passing north fork
the Rosebud changes directions to the east. For the next two and
three-quarter miles the stream flows east through a narrow
valley before it again switches course abruptly, turning back to
the north. The lead battalions of Mills' and Noyes' were nearly
midway between these two bends when word was passed down
to stop. It was 8 A.M.

A benevolent Crook ordered the halt out of consideration for
men and horses, especially the animals who were still showing
signs of fatigue from their 35 mile workout on the 16th.[1] As soon
as the stoppage occurred, hardbittened veterans needed little
incentive or orders to start fires for morning coffee. The men
were allowed to unsaddle their horses and put them out to graze.
Private Towne of F Company, Third Cavalry, remembered they
hobbled the horses to prevent them from stampeding.[2] As the
coffee boiled, men knotted together in small groups to talk or to
tell stories. Others used the rest to lie down on the cool ground
and catch up on sleep. Still others used the time to sit quietly,
light up cigars, or cut thick plugs of tobacco to chew.

Some Crow scouts appeared nervous. Approaching the
General, they reported evidence of Sioux in the area. They told
Crook to keep the men concealed while they examined the
countryside. Pickets were dispatched to hills north of the camp
as a precautionary measure. The remainder of the men enjoyed
the luxury of camp.[3]

The setting where Crook had elected to halt was picturesque.
It lay in a valley one-half mile wide. To the south, towering
bluffs rose 500 feet above the valley floor to dominate the
skyline. North of camp a series of low ridges, fluctuating from
150-800 yards back from the creek, blocked further vision
northward. Beyond these ridges, the treeless prairie sloped
upwards in a broad undulating sweep to the main crest, about a
mile north of the ridges. Here, on the main crest, now known as
Crook's Hill, much of the battle was fought. The main crest

extends for three miles, running roughly from northwest to southeast. A spur ridge comes in one mile west of Crook's Hill and runs at an acute angle southeast for one mile until its termination several hundred yards above the creek, one-half mile east of the west bend. This ridge is known as Royall's Ridge, named in honor of Colonel Royall, whose forces fought over the ground against contending Sioux and Cheyenne. Between Royall Ridge and Crook Hill lies the broad panoramic valley known as Kollmar. The head of Kollmar originates just over one mile west of Crook Hill [Monument Hill on map]. Kollmar parallels Royall Ridge and extends southeast for two miles before emptying into Rosebud Creek at a point midway between the west bend and the Kobold House.[4] Except for the last quarter mile of Kollmar, which is spring-fed, the valley is dry.

It was between the west bend and the Kobold House that Crook had selected to form his morning halt. Captain Anson Mills' battalion of the Third Cavalry, Companies A, E, I, and M, occupied the right bank opposite the Kobold House. Following Mills came the other battalions of the Third Cavalry. Captain Van Vliet's demi-battalion Companies C and G were in the center. Following Van Vliet was the battalion of Captain Guy V. Henry's, Companies B, D, F, and L. On the left bank opposite Mills and resting in the vicinity of the Kobold House was Noyes' Second Cavalry, Companies A, B, D, E, and I. Next in order came the mule-riding infantry of Major Chambers, Companies D and F, Fourth Infantry and Companies C, G and H of the Ninth Infantry. The packers and miners brought up the rear and were still filing into camp, having not yet caught up with the rest of the command.[5]

General Crook parked himself down along the spring near the mouth of Kollmar.[6] Along with his aide, Bourke, and several infantry officers, he became engrossed in a game of whist.[7] It was morning, still cool, but the sun's rays were promising, before the day was done, to supplant the coolness with stifling heat. Some of the soldiers took delight in watching the Shoshones race their horses, Overall, things seemed quiet, deceptively quiet. Sounds of gunfire to the north, faint at first, grew in intensity. By now the officers and men were accustomed to these outbursts and casually discarded them as another episode of scouts acting as if they were enjoying a holiday. The affable Swiss-born Captain Alexander Sutorius dismissed the noise calmly to reporter Finerty, "they are shooting buffaloes over there."[8] But it was soon evident the shots were spreading out in directions suggesting the noise was not the results of a buffalo hunt. It was now 8:30 A.M. Distant gunfire reverberated across the valley.

While Crook relaxed in his camp, his scouts were busy. Leaving Crook, some of the Crows and Shoshones had ventured north to search for their enemy. Eleven miles north of the Rosebud camp they collided with a small force of Sioux and Cheyenne on Corral Creek. At first the allies were able to push aside the miniscule number of warriors. Sparring continued to Ash Creek until the Indians were reinforced from other bands who began to gravitate to the area. Seizing the initiative, the Sioux began to drive the scouts back toward the Rosebud.[9] As the allies retreated towards the Rosebud, the faint sounds of gunfire increased. Suddenly, bursting on the bluffs immediately north of camp, came a score of scouts. Hot on their heels were Indians, by the hundreds. A Shoshone by the name of Limpy, no relation to the Cheyenne of the same name, came tearing down the hillside shouting. "Lakota! Lakota!"[10]

Not only were Sioux and Cheyenne riders coming directly down from the north, but they could be seen riding west and east of the valley. Without waiting for orders, Major George Randall, chief of scouts, hurriedly organized his remaining scouts into a skirmish line on the ridges north of camp. Under Randall's directions, the scouts formed the initial barrier of defense against the Sioux attack. For twenty critical minutes, all that was between the warriors and the troops was a thin band of scouts and a handful of pickets. The warriors closed to within 500 yards of camp. The scouts stood firm and blunted their advance. Resembling a wide arc, Randall's forces extended north and to the east and west in an attempt to cover all avenues of approach.[11] Like a whirlwind charged the Indians. The piercing yells of warriors splintered the air. Flying arrows and the crackling sounds of rifles were everywhere. The Battle of the Rosebud had begun.

The celerity of the Sioux attack bent the line of Randall's, but did not break it. In return the allies regrouped and launched a counterattack, pushing the red wave back. The Battle of the Rosebud can be characterized as a battle of ebb and flow. Charge was met with countercharge. On one such charge, Jack Red Cloud, 18 year old son of the Oglala patriarch, Red Cloud, had his horse killed from underneath him. Indian tradition dictated that he stop and take the bridle from his horse to demonstrate bravery and coolness in the face of danger. Young Red Cloud in his haste to escape ignored the custom. Crow riders reached him and lashed him with their riding quirts to add insult to dishonor. One Crow, leaning down from his pony, snatched Jack's long trailing warbonnet. Another Crow grabbed his rifle and ridiculed the excited young Oglala with verbal chants that he was a boy, and should not be donning a warbonnet. According to Oglala accounts, young Red Cloud was begging for his life, and tears filled his eyes.[12] A number of Sioux, including Crazy Horse, came to his rescue, but not before the youngster had been thoroughly humiliated.[13]

Meanwhile, the camp was a flurry of activity. Officers and sergeants screamed orders. Soldiers scurried for weapons and horses.

Crook was caught flatfooted, not unlike his surprise by Early at Cedar Creek, a dozen years before. Mounting his coal black charger, Crook rode up the bluffs immediately north of Kollmar spring to ascertain exactly what he was up against. His view told him the Indians were in large force and their attacks were emanating from different directions, mainly northeast and west.[14] While Crook was completing his reconnaissance, Captain Nickerson and Lieutenant Colonel Royall were in the process of mobilizing the cavalry for action.[15]

Crook correctly surmized that the key was to wrest the high ground north to strip the advantage now owned by the Sioux. The high bluffs south of camp likewise had to be taken, less the warriors catch the soldiers in a cross fire. Through Captain Nickerson, he instructed Captain Van Vliet's battalion to occupy the commanding summit south of camp. Swinging into action, Van Vliet scaled the steep slopes. Upon topping the bluffs, Van Vliet discovered the top was a broad flat plain. He also discerned that a group of Indians coveted the same objective and were riding madly toward his position from the east end of the ridge top. Van Vliet put his command into formation and advanced toward his foe. Unable to withstand the cavalry charge, the warriors fled, leaving the troopers in sole possession of the high ground.[16] Van Vliet's orders from Crook were to hold his position until further instructions. From his vantage point, the battalion had a ringside seat to the battlefield below.

Facing north Crook's left rested in the vicinity of where the north fork of Rosebud empties into the main stream. Here, at the west bend, Indians were bearing down on the camp and out flanking Randall's scouts. To prevent the Sioux from gaining access to the valley, Henry's battalion was detailed to hold a low mound south of the creek, about 300 yards east of the west bend. Two of Henry's companies, D and F, were rushed up the creek about 500 yards and instructed "to prevent the Indians from turning our supposed left ..."[17] Now that the command's left and rear seemed secure Crook concentrated on the Sioux to the north. The Crows and Shoshones continued to fight valiantly against overwhelming odds. At least two Crows suffered debilitating wounds during the twenty minutes of fighting. One Crow, Bull Snake, was observed by Frank Grouard, leaning against a tree, his thigh shattered, "yelling like a madman exhorting his warrior friends to fight on."[18] The other wounded Crow was Fox-Just-Coming-Over-Hill, later renamed Old Coyote.[19]

Crook sent, in support of the allies, two of his infantry companies. Major Chambers directed Companies G and H, under Captains Burrowes and Burt, to dismount and take the ridges immediately north of the spring.[20] To the west of Burt and Burrowes, the remaining three companies of infantry, Companies D and F of the Fourth under Captains Cain and Luhn respectively, along with Company C, Ninth Infantry, commanded by Captain Samuel Munson, marched north as dismounted skirmishers. Further to the left, on the flank of the three infantry units, moved the miners and packers.

Lieutenant Thaddeus Capron, serving with Munson on the right of Luhn, claimed the orders to move out came none too soon " . . . for the Indians came charging in upon us in large numbers."[21] Aide-de-camp Nickerson accompanied the infantry and recorded his feelings concerning their adversaries:

> Many wore the long Sioux war bonnet of eagle's plumes, which floated and fluttered in the air, back of the wearer, to the distance of five or six feet; while others wore half masks of the heads of wild animals with the ears and sometimes the horns, still protruding, giving them the appearance of devils from the nether world, or uncouth demons from the hills of Brocken . . . The warriors dashed here, there, everywhere; up and down in ceaseless activity; their gaudy decorations, wearing plumes and glittering arms, forming a panoramic view of barbaric splendor, once seen, never to be forgotten.[22]

The advance of the three companies, D and F of the Fourth and C of the Ninth, all under the authority of Captain Cain, moved northward in skirmish line formation. Unable to withstand the long-range firepower of the Springfield rifles of the infantry, the

Lakotas slipped eastward, their attacks now erupting from a natural gap in the main crest. In support of Cain's advance, Captain Noyes' battalion of the Second Cavalry, with the exception of Captain Dewee's company, which remained in the bottom as horse holders, moved forward as skirmishers on Cain's right flank.[23]

The combined infantry-cavalry skirmish line was now over a mile long. Noyes' battalion pushed northward, up the rolling ground which was bare of any fire cover. Noyes' route took him toward the main crest a mile north of the camp and was focused on an area now dubbed the "gap." The gap was a three hundred yard innate break in the main crest. It also served as a natural and convenient avenue for attack in the breaks surrounding the Rosebud Valley. At the outset of the battle, the Sioux and Cheyenne had poured through to fight the bluecoats. The left of the gap formed the terminus of Crook's Hill. To the right or east of the opening, the crest angled southeast for three-quarters of a mile before terminating some 300 yards from the creek. The terrain east of the gap provided excellent protection. Large boulders, sandstone crevices, rimrocks, and pine studded slopes could be utilized to maximum advantage.

It was toward this natural orifice that Noyes spearheaded his cavalry-foot soldiers. In support of him, came Burt and Burrowes' companies. They were proceeding beyond Noyes' column to become the right flank.[24]

While the infantry and Noyes were manuevering into position, the Sioux were expanding their theater of operations to the west. Their endeavors were blunted by the combined efforts of the scouts and pickets. Moving around the flanks of the Crows and Shoshones, they attempted to stampede the horses in the Valley. Captain Henry's two companies and the three companies of Cain checked their progress.[25]

Checking this advance, Cain was now free to concentrate on the main crest. Henry's two companies remained stationary south of the creek, doing good work in repelling Indian forays coming down the Rosebud.[26]

Meanwhile, the other half of the warriors poured through the gap and attacked directly from the north. They utilized the rocky outcroppings and pines east of the gap for defense. Thwarted by Cain's infantry, they now watched as Noyes and the two companies of Burt and Burrowes advanced toward them. Small knots of Sioux would venture out in front of the lines only to disappear when the soldiers bullets indicated they had found the range. Then, when one of the anxious troopers got too far out in front of support, the warriors would suddenly turn on their quarry and drive them back on the main line. At one point, near the gap, Burt and Burrowes attempted to lure some Cheyennes into ambush. Crows and Shoshones acting as inviting bait, sallied forth. The infantry waited patiently to spring the trap. The ruse failed when some of the Cheyennes of White Elk's band became suspicious. They saw the trick and backed off before the trap could be sprung.[27]

It was during one of these daring charges and countercharges that one of many individual deeds of heroism was recorded in the Battle of the Rosebud. Near the center of the gap, a Cheyenne warrior by the name of Comes-in-Sight was rescued from certain death. Of heroic acts that chronicle the rich and colorful history of the Cheyenne people, none is more poignant or dramatic as this episode. A bullet from the carbine or rifle from one of Crook's men had dropped Comes-In-Sight's mount. Afoot and alone, he looked like easy prey for the scouts who closed in for the coup de grace. Suddenly, from out of nowhere, dashed an unknown zigzagging rider. The would-be rescuer beckoned for Comes-In-Sight to climb up behind. Bullets kicked up earth around the horse, but none hit their mark. Other warriors, including Crazy Horse, watched from a distance, too far removed to be of any assistance except vocally.[28] Swinging himself up behind his savior, Comes-In-Sight escaped. The person who so gallantly ignored the perils of the situation was none other than the sister of Comes-In-Sight, Buffalo-Calf-Road-Woman. For her act of individual bravery, the Cheyennes recall with much pride the Battle of the Rosebud as the battle "Where the Girl Saved Her Brother."[29]

Owing to the similarity of dress between the scouts and the Sioux, the infantrymen experienced difficulty in differentiating between friend and foe. The allies had been issued strips of red cloth to tie to their arms to accentuate the differences. Later, the scouts would bitterly complain that soldiers had been shooting at them.[30]

Although the fight was far from over, a feeling of confidence was returning to Crook. He had overcome the surprise attack without too much damage, save perhaps to his ego and pride. His skirmish line north of the creek was progressing steadily, if slowly, toward the summit. However, there was still one nemesis, mainly the warriors who occupied the ridge crest east of the gap. Their combined firepower had pinned down the advancing units of cavalry and infantry. Now was the time for offensive actions that only a lightning cavalry charge could produce. Crook still had not played all his cards. He still held an ace in the hole. Mills' four companies had not been deployed in battle. Could they be the hammer blow to break the Sioux resistance and turn the tide of battle?

CHAPTER VII

"The Best Cavalry on Earth"

When the firing commenced, Captain Anson Mills mounted his horse and rode to the high promontory south of camp. The bluffs afforded him a spectacular crow's-nest view of the surrounding area. Mills later recalled, "I saw on the crest of the horizon about two miles distance, great numbers of moving objects, looking somewhat like distant crows silhouetted on the clear sky above the horizon. I soon came to the conclusion that they were Indians in great number."[1] Mills quickly returned to his battalion, instructing them to "saddle up, there — saddle up, there, quick!"[2]

He received orders through Major Evans, "to mount, cross the stream and charge and drive the Indians from the opposite hills," meaning the ridges east of the gap. Mills formed his battalion south of the creek. To augment Mills Companies B and L from Henry's battalion were temporarily assigned to him.

Mills assembled his six companies in the bottom and to the right rear of Noyes' skirmishers. The honor of leading the column advance fell to Lieutenant Lawson Company A, followed in succession by Companies E (Sutorius), M (Paul), I (Andrews), B (Meinhold), and L (Vroom). In a line of four columns deep, covering a front 200-300 yards wide, they charged up the southeastern slope of the ridge, east of the gap.[3] The pace was too rapid to render carbines effective. Most of the men resorted to revolvers to fire into the warriors concealed amongst the rocks and timber. Mills' troopers broke into wild cheers as they raced pell mell toward the Sioux. Warriors scrambled to get out of the way, retreating up the slope to the crest itself. Upon reaching the line of rocks, just vacated by the Sioux, Mills ordered his men to dismount and advance on foot. Mills later recounted:

> These Indians were most hideous, every one being painted in most hideous colors and designs, stark naked except their moc-casins, breech clouts and head gear, the latter consisting of feathers and horns; some of the horses being also painted, and the Indians proved then and there that they were the best cavalry soldiers on earth. In charging up towards us they exposed little of their person, hanging on with one arm around the neck and one leg over the horse, firing and lancing from underneath the horses' necks so that there was no part of the Indians at which we could aim.[4]

Mills' charge took the Indians by flank and front. The aston-ished warriors could not brace up under such a devastating attack. Lakotas scattered in every direction, but largely along the ridge top west. The thunderbolt charge completely cleared tribesmen from positions east of the gap.

The impetus of the attack allowed the dismounted cavalry of Noyes to move forward, now free from Indian fire which had kept his troopers pinned down. Because of the distance involved, infantry of Chambers and the cavalry of Noyes could do nothing but watch the fleeing warriors shift their position along the crest from right to left. Chambers and Noyes were too far away to pour an effective enfilading fire into their ranks.

The Indian retreat did not stop until reaching the summit of Crook's Hill one mile west of the gap.[5] From this new vantage point, they fired long-range at the bluecoats advancing on foot toward them.

The demeanor on Crook's face remained expressionless. He seldom exhibited outward emotion, but inside burned a rage to succeed. He certainly felt a shift in the battle to the side of the army. Sensing stability in the crisis, all he needed now to gain control was to secure the high ground upon which the warriors had withdrawn. Crook ordered Mills to reform his men and "to take that hill" referring to what is now Crook's Hill.[6] The attack over the broken terrain east of the gap had disrupted Mills' organization. Bringing his troopers back down from the ground they had just seized, Mills quickly reformed for a charge on Crook's Hill.

While Mills was in the valley forming for his second charge, Colonel Royall observed warriors posted on a ridge immediately south of Kollmar Creek. Royall, without informing Mills or the commander, commandeered the rear three companies of Mills' command and led them in headlong pursuit west. With his three remaining companies, Mills again took them on a thunderous cavalry charge, this time his target Crook's Hill. With Mills in front, Companies A, E, and M converged on the warriors.[7] Indian resistance melted in the face of the demonic yelling bluecoated troopers. The Sioux retreated westward along the level summit of the crest for three quarters a mile, finally stopping at the next rise now known as Conical Hill. Halting at Crook's Hill, Mills reformed his men for another attack, his objective being the warriors on Conical Hill. Just as he was about to charge, General Crook arrived and ordered him to "advance no further" but instead to dismount and form a skirmish line.[8]

Now that he had possession of the high ground on either side of the creek, Crook was content to consolidate his forces and ponder his next move and that of his elusive adversary. Clearly, he had wrested the iniative away from the Indians, yet, to continue pursuring the warriors as Mills had demonstrated twice, would prove to be a futile exercise. Crook and Mills were joined on the crest within minutes by the huffing and puffing infantry and miners.

Four hundred yards northwest of Crook's Hill is a large sandstone outcropping. Civilian miners, packers, and a handful of infantrymen were sent out to control this rocky ledge called Packers Rock. They would act as a deterrent against further Indians raids that might spawn from Conical Hill. Warriors exchanged long-range firing with the hodgepodge force, but neither side meant to do anything other than deter against surprise attack from the other.

It was now a little past 9:30 A.M. Crook inventoried the battlefield. Miners and packers held the northwestern rim of the defense posted at Packers Rock. On the southside of the level plateau flanking Packers Rock, a score of men occupied the southern edge of the crest at a site now dubbed Packers Ridge. The men at Packers Ridge faced westward gazing down the broad valley of Kollmar. On the southwest crest where Crook established headquarters were the three cavalry companies of Mills. In the center of Crook's Hill from left to right were posted the infantry companies of Cain, Luhn, and Munson. To the right of Munson, Noyes' Second Cavalry held the long sloping ridge down to the gap. On Munson's right were Companies B, I, and E of the Second. Company E was positioned on the left of the gap. Opposite the gap was Company D.[9] Captain Dewees and Company A were in the valley bringing up the battalion horses. The companies of Burt and Burrowes were under a similar mission.[10]

Surgeons established a field hospital on the south slope of Crook's Hill. Casualties to this point were minimal. Several men had been wounded from Cain's and Noyes' troops. Burt collected the wounded and brought them to the hill.[11] Crook's Hill was secure, as was the right, which stretched down to the gap. In fact there were no Indians, opposing the men of Noyes at all.

If Crook was content with the defensive alignment atop Crook's Hill, he was less than pleased with the action to the west.

He realized he was fighting a battle on a very broad front, nearly three miles wide. While the troops on Crook's Hill were in no danger, he fretted over the separation of Royall's command. Five companies, one-third of the cavalry, were a mile away.

CHAPTER VIII

Royall Goes A'Chasing Indians

The open valley of Kollmar Creek separated Royall from Crook. Mindful that the commands should be united, Crook sent a courier after Royall with instructions to recall his advance and rejoin the forces concentrating on Crook's Hill.

When Royall detached the three companies from Mills' battalion, he moved westward over the southern slope overlooking Kollmar. This ridge is now known as Royall Ridge. Meeting Henry and his two companies, he ordered the captain to join him. Royall's five companies consisted of 225 officers and men. As with Mills on the right, the Indians evaporated in the face of the advancing cavalry, only to resurrect themselves on the next adjacent ridge. The ardor of the enlisted men vent itself in cheers. The Indians were on the run.[2] The officers, too, were caught up in the uncontrollable urge to catch the fleeing warriors. Pursuit is laudable, but it has to be directed, and it has to produce expected results or it is all in vain. Royall's movement, so far removed from the rest of Crook's force, was resolving nothing. As the battle progressed, Royall's sortie was going to have severe ramifications on the outcome of the fight on the Rosebud.

Spearheading the chase was Andrews' company. Andrews route took him a mile west of Crook's Hill. The Indians then divided their forces into two groups, one party going west, while the other band continued to stay just ahead of Andrews' column. Lieutenant James Foster and 18 men were detached from Andrews' command and ordered to "clear those people on the left away."[3] The Sioux occupied a post to the west, which, if left ignored, would permit the Indians to flank the command.[4]

Foster complied by driving the warriors from ridge top to ridge top. However, his route separated him still further from Royall until he was a mile beyond support. Seeing the smallness of his column, Indians concentrated on his force in hopes of cutting him off and destroying him. Luckily for Foster, his superior, Captain Andrews, on a rocky ledge to the north, saw his predicament. Although Andrews was unable to bring his forces over for support because of a deep chasm dividing them, he did manage to send a messenger through to instruct Foster to rejoin the main command. The courier, Private Herbert Weaver, raced up to Foster with the message to fall back.[5]

Foster, by this time, was also aware of his peril. He suddenly discovered warriors closing in on him from both flanks. Retiring swiftly, and in good order, he managed to return to Royall with only the wounding of two men.[6]

Andrews, too, had been a victim of the thrilling chase. His platoon of men had outdistanced the other cavalry by nearly one-half mile. Finally, Royall came to a conclusion that further pursuit was an exercise in futility and called a halt to the game the Lakota seemed to be enjoying. He summoned Andrews to withdraw from his advanced and unsupported position and return to the main command. As Andrews retired, Indians quickly took up his vacated position.

Colonel Royall had ordered the halt and the concentration of the battalion at the head of Kollmar Creek. This site is now known as Royall's first position. It is located one mile west of Crook's Hill.

Royall's position was located at the eastern end of a series of rocky knobs and ledges. The western end of the ridge where

Andrews had stopped is now called Andrews Point and is a half miles west of Royall's first position.

The fighting up to this point was characterized by one of Royall's officers as:

> Nothing had been accomplished by our repeated charges except to drive the Sioux from one crest, to immediately reappear upon the next . . . Nothing tangible seemed to be gained by prolonging the contest. When we took a crest, no especial advantage accrued by occupying it, and the Sioux ponies always outdistanced our grain-fed American horses in the race for the next one.[7]

It did not take the warriors long to understand that Royall's troopers, separated as they were, might be easily beaten decisively in detail before aid from the soldiers to the east could arrive. Here lay a golden opportunity for the insurgents to concentrate on an isolated column and perhaps achieve the same success to the remainder of the bluecoats with Crook.

Approximately 500 warriors converged on Royall. They laid down a defilading fire from the north, west, and south. However, the soldier carbines were able to keep the warriors at bay. Three times the Indians charged and each time they were beaten back.[8] The action at Royall's first position lasted for nearly two hours.

While Royall was engaging Sioux at the head of Kollmar Creek, Crook's first courier, Captain Azor Nickerson, reached the beleagured troopers. Bullets perforated the earth beneath the captain's horse as he reigned in his mount in front of Royall.[9] Crook's message was short and terse to "extend . . . right and connect with the left of the main body."[10] Royall meekly complied with the directive. He sent the solitary company of Captain Meinhold to link up with Crook. Colonel Royall maintained in his report written shortly after the battle that he could not retreat because of the pressure being exerted on him by the large warrior force facing him.[11] Reporter Davenport agreed with Royall's assertions by adding, "to retreat into the hollow [Kollmar] on the right . . . was to risk the certain loss of nearly the whole battalion."[12]

Under examination, the logic of Royall and Davenport is not substantiated by the facts. Meinhold got through relatively unscathed, loosing one trooper wounded and one horse killed.[13] The wounded soldier, Private Henry Steiner, received a painful gunshot wound to the shoulder which fractured his scapula.[14] Meinhold's safe passage should serve as ample proof that the five companies could have, in all probability, gotten through in the same manner. Why Royall did not immediately elect to retire with his entire command must remain one of the battle's major puzzlements. Futhermore, the withdrawal of Meinhold was utterly meaningless. It reduced Royall's force by 20%, and it was to become painfully evident that he would need every available person to hold his position. Nor was the dispatching of Meinhold, in any stretch of the imagination, perceived as a conduit to link up the two separated units. The departure of Meinhold forced Royall to stretch out his already thin defense to cover the vacated area.

The arrival of Meinhold on Crook's Hill did nothing to ease Crook's troubled mind. He dispatched another courier to Royall, requesting they return. It was now 10:30 A.M.[15] Meanwhile, an impatient Crook, was annoyed over the indecisiveness of the engagement. To pursue was indeed pointless.[16] For as much as Royall's reasons for not immediately linking with Crook are incredulous, the next decision by Crook mortgaged any hope of victory.

Crook was convinced in his own mind that the warriors could only be fighting so fiercely out of protection for their nearby encampment.

Preparatory to a general advance, the General decided to disengage his cavalry on Crook's Hill and push them down the valley to secure the Indian camp. Summoning Captain Mills, he admonished him: "It is time to stop this skirmishing, Colonel.

You must take your battalion and go for their village away down the canyon."[17] Meanwhile Crook would wait with his infantry for Royall.

Crook's decision to withdraw over one-half of his cavalry force, in search of an unconfirmed village, would constitute the other half of the major cause for the battle's dismal outcome.[18]

The departure of Mills from the crest was observed by the warriors. It is highly likely the Indians interpreted the troop withdrawal as the start of a general retreat. Nothing inspired a Plains Indians so much as seeing the backs of his foe. The withdrawal of Mills signaled a furious assault by the warriors against Royall to further drive a wedge between the two separated columns of soldiers.[19]

Two distinct fights were developing. On the left, Royall was hotly engaged. Upon receipt of the second message to join Crook, Royall endeavored to comply. But he had waited too long. Warriors shifted their position and sealed off the escape route utilized by Meinhold. From his posture at the head of Kollmar, Royall's next move was to retire south to the crest of a long ridge south of Kollmar. Led horses were sent in advance to afford them better protection. Soldiers, following in the footsteps of the mounts, were compelled to fend off bold charges from their attackers. The retrograde movement covered one-half mile without loss. Royall's second position occupied the western edge of the crest at the point where it drops off precipitously to a wide and deep chasm. Formerly, this valley had been the route of Foster's escape following the Indians attempt to encircle him. To the south, the crest sloped down in a fairly level pattern. The entire area was void of any protective fire covering except along the lip of the deep chasm. Here, sandstone rocks offered some protection.

Defensively, Royall posted Captains Andrews and Vroom on the north slope to face their first position, now occupied by warriors.[20] Captain Henry with the two remaining companies, D and F, were dispatched south of the slope and ordered to take cover in the sandstone rocks bordering the deep chasm. Henry's timely arrival negated Indians attempting to ouflank the soldiers by occupying the same rocks.[21]

While warriors occupied Royall, another force of Indians, the second prong of the Sioux and Cheyenne attack, concentrated on the troops on Crook's Hill. Pouring forth from Conical Hill, Indians made a hell-bent for leather charge straight down the valley of Kollmar. Their attack swept by the flank of packers and soldiers on Packers Ridge, past Crook Hill, and to the very mouth of Kollmar where the soldiers had been camped in the morning. There were no troopers available to contest the intrepid Sioux and Cheyenne advance.

The assault surprised a Shoshone boy herding some of the scout's horses near the spring. The young Shoshone was quickly killed. A Sioux scalped him, leaving only a trace of hair along the nape of the neck.[22]

Crook could do nothing. Only the fortuitous approach of one of Captain Van Vliet's companies stalled the warriors advance. By chance, Van Vliet was in progress of joining Crook on the main crest. Van Vliet had been ordered to unite with Crook to take the place of the departed cavalry going down the Rosebud.[23]

To neutralize the ferocity of the Sioux, Crook sent his idle scouts into action. Major Randall assembled the Crows on the southwest rim. Meanwhile, Crook's aid, Bourke, received permission to lead the Shoshone delegation on the foray from the crest. With Bourke and Randall leading, the allies charged into the flank of the retiring warriors. The attack drove the yelling redmen in confusion.[24] In a little swale south and west of Conical Hill, the Indians halted to meet their attackers. Both sides dismounted for hand to hand combat. The fighting was brisk. Overmatched, the Sioux retreated westward along the crest, not stopping until they were beyond Andrews Point nearly two miles west of Crook's Hill. Lieutenant Bourke continued the pursuit with only a handful of scouts until he and his followers, so engrossed in the exhiliarating chase, had not realized they had outstripped their support. In fact, the balance of the scouts were returning to Crook's line.

Halting at Andrews Point, Bourke, with his bugler, Elmer Snow, Company M Third Cavalry, took heed of their situation. They were alone and abandoned with Lakota closing the gap between then. About the same time that Bourke noticed the Indians converging on him, a messenger from Randall arrived with a note to withdraw.[25] Bourke and Snow beat a hasty retreat with the Sioux in close pursuit. So near were the Indians that Bourke emptied the contents of his carbine into the charging warriors at a distance of thirty yards before giving spurs to his horse.[26] Snow was less fortunate. Indian bullets tore through his extremities and Snow was "badly shot through both arms near the elbows."[27] Miraculously, both escaped the grasp of the Sioux and safely returned to their line.[28]

A similar incident was experienced by Sergeant Van Moll who accompanied Randall and the Crows. Van Moll's enthusiasm had likewise taken him far beyond the realm of friends. He was without the benefit of horse. The attackers succeeded in cutting him off. Were it not for the heroic efforts of a Crow by the name of Humpy, Van Moll would have certainly been killed. Humpy saw the soldier's plight. He rushed back to him, exhorting the trooper to mount behind him. Van Moll needed little encouragement. Climbing aboard, the two scampered away, eluding their would-be antagonist.[29]

Troopers from Crook's Hill stared at the unlikely pair of heroes as they dashed for the sanctuary of the crest. They were an odd couple, what with the misshapened form of Humpy and long-legged Van Moll astride the back of a diminutive pony. The gangly legs of Van Moll nearly touched the ground, observed Finerty.[30]

The return of the Crows and Shoshones occurred around 11

A.M. The charge had been beneficial, for it had sufficiently disrupted the Lakota's aggressive nature and "prevented further deterioration of the army's situation."[31] While Bourke was at Andrews Point he managed to size up the predicament of Royall. He was able to report to the General that gyrating Sioux were converging on Royall from three sides.[32]

Following the scout's attack, a steady fire from warriors posted on Conical Hill became a concern. To minimize their disruption, Crook unleashed his infantry with orders to "drive the Indians from our front."[33] From left to right the companies of Cain, Luhn, and Munson advanced in skirmish formation toward Conical Hill. The level plateau connecting Crook's Hill with Conical Hill which the infantry had to traverse afforded no protective features. Under the command of Captain Cain, the line moved forward jauntily and in good military order.

Company D occupied the left with its flank secure on the south slope overlooking Kollmar valley. To the right of Cain and forming the center was Company F under Captain Luhn. Company C, Ninth Infantry, under Captain Samuel Munson, anchored the right with its flank bordering the north slope of the high plateau.[34]

Although the warriors had a clear field of fire, their shots went errant. Failing to halt the progress of the soldiers, the Indians abandoned their position when the infantrymen came within 400 yards of Conical Hill. At that point, a fusillade of lead from the Springfield rifles sent the warriors scurring. The infantry attack gave clear and concise evidence that the rigid discipline and organization of the army was far superior to the highly individualistic fighting style of the Plains Indian. But the attack was barren of results, save for the taking of an unimportant piece of Montana real estate. The infantry remained in possession of the ground for a short time before being recalled to Crook's Hill.[35] Corresponding to Cain's advance was the withdrawal of Van Vliet's battalion south of the Rosebud. Van Vliet arrived around 11:30 A.M. taking up the slack by the departing Mills and the three infantry companies in the Conical Hill sortie.[36]

For the time being, conditions on Crook's Hill had stabilized. Long-range firing occasionally spat mushrooms of dust from whining bullets impacting into the hard Montana gumbo.

Captain Burt rode up to Crook and queried: "General, many say that they get so hardened to this sort of thing [the constant firing of battle] that they don't mind it, and I often wonder whether you feel like I do in a position of this kind?"

Showing little motion Crook retorted, "How do you feel?" "Why, just as though, if you were not in sight, I'd be running like hell," was Burt's response.

"Well, I feel exactly that way myelf," Crook replied.[37]

Although not expressed, that same sentiment was probably on the mind of Royall and his battalion. An ever-concerned Crook sent another courier to his second in command urging him to join up. There, things were not stable, if anything, they were rapidly disintegrating. Royall found a worsening condition at his second position. The ferocity from Lakota assaults predicated he dismount his troopers and deploy in a line of skirmishers.[38] In this manner he planned to retire toward Crook's position. To protect the led horses, they were placed on the south slope of Royall's Ridge facing east. Not counting his horse holders, Royall could muster only 150 cavalrymen to stem the red tide which seemed to roll in from every direction except east. Royall was cognizant of the fact that even this avenue of escape, east-ward along the ridge top, would not last indefinitely. It would only be a question of time before the Indians would seal off this route, too. The mile-long retreat would be slow and tedious. With the exception of a three hundred yard break, a half mile east of the seond position, the ridge was continuous. Royall's stratagem was to proceed along the ridge which overlooked Kollmar until he was south and directly opposite Crook. Then the time would be ripe for him to mount his battalion and make

the break for the crest. The problem with the strategy was that
Kollmar is much wider at the head of the valley than at its
mouth. Near the mouth, the valley tapers down to a deep gulch,
affording an opponent the opportunity to fire into the battalion's
ranks without being exposed to return fire.

Royall pondered his move. He could charge into the Indians,
growing in numbers to the north. He could probably push them
aside, but casualties would surely be high. He opted instead, to
retire in an orderly fashion and make the break underneath
Crook.

The third phase of Royall's movement began around 11:30
A.M. Vroom's Company L took the advance, placing itself along
the north slope of the ridge overlooking Kollmar. Behind
Vroom's force came Captain Andrews' I Company. On the
opposite slope and parallel with Vroom and Andrews were
Henry's companies, D and F. Royall's shift was perceived by the
Lakota who "from every ridge, rock, and sagebrush, . . . poured
a galling fire upon the retiring battalion . . . They seemed,
indeed, to spring up instantaneously as if by magic, in front, in
rear and upon both flanks."[39] In one instance of Indian tenacity,
they came so close to the retiring bluecoats on the north slope
that a Cheyenne by the name of Limpy had his horse shot out
from underneath.[40] Several cavalrymen, seeing his defenseless
posture, attempted to administer a coup d'etat. Realizing Limpy's predicament, Young Two Moon, nephew of Two Moon,
raced toward his friend. Owing to Limpy's deformity, he had
one leg shorter than the other because of a birth defect, he could
not easily mount behind his companion. Nearby were some
unusual sandstone rocks, standing alone as sentinels in the valley
of Kollmar. Limpy made his way over to the rocks and climbed
up. Young Two Moon made another pass. Leaping from his
perch, Limpy firmly seated himself behind his rescuer and sped
away before the soldiers could draw an accurate bead on either
of them.[41]

Coming to the break in the ridge, Royall expected to encounter strong resistance. Surprisingly, the Indians only harassed his flanks. The troopers pushed on, reaching the continuation of the ridge. The horses were passed over to the north slope of Royall Ridge and down into the valley of Kollmar. Less than three fourths of a mile would mark the distance required before saddling up and riding out. Finally the time arrived. Crook's Hill was directly north.[42] To proceed further east would be pointless and take the battalion away from Crook. The horses were collected in a side ravine of Kollmar running from the north.[43]

The Indians were sensing something was about to happen and renewed their attacks with great vigor. The command found itself under a galling fire from three directions. It was impossible to abandon the ridge top lest the warriors trap them in the bottom of the narrow ravine. Royall summoned his adjutant, Lieutenant Lemly, and instructed him to ride to Crook with an urgent plea for assistance.[44]

A reticent Crook exhibited no outward emotion to Lemly's plea from Royall. Indeed, nothing ever seemed to rattle his rock-solid countenance. Earlier in the battle, he had his horse shot out from under him, with little telling affect. But inwardly, the veteran Civil War campaigner and Indian fighter must have known that the departure of Mills was now a serious error. He had underestimated the fighting prowess of the Sioux and overestimated the ability of Royall to extricate himself from his dilemma. A reluctant Crook had no recourse but to scrap his plans of sending Mills down the valley. The village would have to wait. Crook sent his aide Nickerson after Mills with the somber order to return to the main column and abort the village-hunting mission. Crook wasted little time in sending the infantry companies of Burt and Burrowes to Royall's support.[45]

Indians surrounded Royall on three sides, from the west, south, and now the east. The attackers must be driven from the ridge top in order to make a break for the horses. Vroom's company, in the lead, was ordered along the crest to drive the bold warriors back. Hopefully, this would buy some precious time for the remaining companies to get to their animals.[46]

Correspondent Davenport, writing for the *New York Herald*, and the only reporter accompanying Royall, calculated that the lives of a few troopers would have to be sacrificed in order to extricate the balance of the command.[47]

Vroom had hardly established a foothold on the crest when Sioux and Cheyenne forces quickly surrounded the hopelessly outnumbered company. Royall countermanded his decision to go to the horses. Captain Henry and the other troops of cavalry were ordered into the center of the maelstrom in an attempt to extricate Vroom. Henry was the first to arrive. His quick action saved Vroom from an even rougher handling. As it was, Vroom, in the brief span that he was isolated, had five men killed and three wounded, a casualty rate of over 30% for the entire engagement.[48]

The four companies formed a 325 yard long skirmish line atop what is now known as Royall's third position.[49] Lakota angled in from all directions but seemed strongest from the northwest and southwest. The battalion was caught in an enfilading fire. Warriors showed reckless abandon as they catapulted toward the beleaguered troopers. One warrior was dropped within 50 yards of the line.[50]

From various estimates made by the officers, the combined firepower of the Lakota and Cheyenne in this attack was between 500-700.[52] Royall's defensive force barely exceeded 100, since every fourth man was detailed to hold horses.

The situation was tense. Officers and non-commissioned personnel urged the men to stand firm, less they be overrun.

One sergeant, John Shingle of Company I, had been relegated to guard the horses of the dismounted companies. Unable to watch the battle build, and not be a participant, he finally succumbed to his inner feelings. Bolting from his mundane duty, he gave his responsibilities to another sergeant, and rushed to the crest. Reaching the fighting on the ridge, Shingle was heard over the din of battle, "Face them men! —face them!"[52]

One officer was heard to cry out, "Great God, men, don't go back on the Old Third!" The wavering line responded. Facing the ridge top, they drove the warriors from the crest.[53]

Davenport later wrote that the Indians ponies were so close that the muzzle blasts from soldiers' carbines singed the animals' nostrils or blackened them.[54]

Captain Guy V. Henry, the gallant and popular officer of the Third, was astride his horse near the southern edge of the crest exhorting his men to stand their ground, when he was suddenly struck in the face with a .44 caliber bullet. The projectile penetrated the skin below the left eye, tearing through the fleshy upper part of the mouth and under the nose, finally coming out from his face beneath the right eye.[55] The stunned Henry swayed in his saddle, blood filling his mouth and covering his face in the process. He slumped off his horse, falling prostrate onto the ground.[56]

Several different versions have been recorded. Davenport claims Henry did not fall from his horse, maintaining instead, Henry's troopers lifted him from his horse and led the stricken officer to the rear.[57] Another account reported in the *Army-Navy Journal,* July 22, 1876, indicates Henry never lost his seat. A trooper led his horse to the rear.[58]

That Henry fell to the earth seems most likely, considering that many accounts report that soldiers and scouts hurried to shield his body from the onslaught of Lakota warriors who rushed to count coup upon the lifeless corpse. When Henry went down, his orderly was also hit. But before the jubilant Sioux could adminster the final rites to the pair, a contingent of soldiers, Crows and Shoshones, reached the stricken captain.[59] Just who should receive credit for first reaching Henry is a matter of conjecture. Shoshone accounts give the honor to Tigee.[60] Plenty Coups said a charge by Crows saved Henry from death.[61] Still other reports credit troopers from Henry's own Company D with saving his life. Whoever it was, they reached his limp body just prior to the Sioux. The bevy of soldiers and scouts shielding his body, fired at point blank range into the mass of warriors approaching, driving the Lakota back in disarray.

Henry was assisted to his feet and placed back on his horse. Later, when the surgeon examined Henry's wounds, they were first pronounced as fatal. Blood congealed on his face. He could not see and he could not talk above a faint whisper. Breathing was difficult. Amazingly, Henry's constitution was stronger than the severe wound. The stoic captain whispered to the attending surgeon who bent over to dress his wounds, "Fix me up so that I can go back."[62] Despite the gravity of the wounds, he recovered, although he permanently lost sight in his left eye.

The wounding of Henry marks the time when Royall's troopers finally made the break to join Crook. In disorder, the troops raced down the slope of Royall Ridge to the waiting horses in Kollmar. Victorious warriors reached the summit of the ridge and poured in a deadly fire which further panicked the cavalrymen. Lakota to the north raked the command with an oblique fire. The infantry support Crook sent to aid Royall saw the ghastly scene developing and raced pell mell down from the hill to get into supporting position.

Company F, Third Cavalry, under the command of Lieutenant Banbridge Reynolds, son of Colonel Joseph Reynolds, appears to have suffered the brunt of the casualties on the retreat. Sergeant David Marshall and several enlisted men became separated from their horses. The Indians encircled them. Left to fend for themselves, according to eyewitness accounts, they were seen using their carbines as clubs. Farrier Gerald O'Grady, observing Marshall's demise, returned to give assistance. Although he arrived too late to save his life, he did manage to bring his body off the field before it could be mutilated.[63] Another private, Phineas Towne, helped carry the mortally wounded Marshall from the field until he, too, was hit in the abdomen by a warrior bullet.[64]

One unfortunate private, probably Gilbert Roe, was observed surrendering his carbine to an angry warrior. Davenport, writing in the *New York Herald,* July 6, 1876, said the warrior "flung it [the carbine] to the ground and cleft his head with a stroke of the tomahawk."[65]

A trooper in Company I, William Allen, a twenty year veteran, had his horse shot during the retreat. Dismounted, he looked like easy prey. Raising his carbine, he began to return the fire directed at him. Allen finally went down in a flurry of Sioux bullets. Still alive, he drew his pistol to continue the uneven match until a warrior drew near enough to brain him to death.[66]

Crow and Shoshone who had come to the aid of the sticken troopers appear to have brought up the rear of the column behind Reynolds' company. They displayed uncommon valor and courage. Reaching the panicky cavalrymen in the bottom of Kollmar at the critical moment when the men were trying to mount, they organized a defensive line, which discouraged the Lakota from wandering too close to their lines. Following Company F out of the ravine, several of the scouts were seen, waving joyously, two fresh and bloody scalps.[67] With the unrelenting Sioux at their heels, they accompanied the bluecoats down the steep side of Kollmar Creek.[68] "Many soldiers, even companies, owe their survival to the brave Crows and Shoshones."[69] Without a doubt, sufficient credit is not given the allies for their role in the Battle of the Rosebud.

Sharing honors with the allies in saving Royall must go to the infantry charging down from Crook's Hill. Burt and Burrowes raced down from the hilltop to occupy a low crown knob 600 yards north of Kollmar and slightly northeast of Royall's third position. Burt and Burrowes arrived at this ridge about the same time Royall was making the break to the horses. Burt reported, "we dismounted and moved forward at double time and on reaching the ridge stopped the Indians quickly and decisively without loss on our part."[70] Burt was certain that his command had "disabled two Indians and three ponies."[71] The wounded Henry gave high praise to the work of the infantry. Henry declared, "During the retreat we were saved from greater loss by the charge of two infantry companies . . ."[72] Echoing Henry's comments was infantry captain Luhn. Luhn wrote, "Royall would have had hard time of it" were it not for their interceding.[73] And the correspondent for the *New York Graphic* simply credits the arrival of the two infantry companies with saving Royall's battalion from destruction.[74]

After mounting their horses in Kollmar, the cavalrymen were compelled to run a gauntlet of fire for 300 yards before they could ascend the north bank of Kollmar. Royall passed to the east of Burt and Burrowes and joined the command on Crook's Hill. Royall, along with his adjutant Lemly and Lieutenant Foster, had narrow escapes.[75] Lemly reported Royall was the last man to mount the slope and leave the scene of carnage.[76]

The battalion was placed into the line which Noyes had occupied in the morning. It was now 1 P.M.

The action with Royall at his third position was not the only fighting occurring. Warriors from Conical Hill became active. Angling southeast down Kollmar, they sliced at the civilians and soldiers situated along Packers Ridge. Infantry, packers, and miners from their position now swung west to give them a volley of lead. Warriors nearly succeeded in overrunning the position on Packers Ridge.[77]

The boldness of the Indians along this front prevented Crook from sending further reinforcements to Royall. Checked by the infantry on Crook's Hill, the Indians reassembled on Conical Hill for another assault. They were just in the process of charging when Mills was seen emerging out of the valley of the Rosebud. Mills' presence on their rear forced the warriors to forgo their plans on Crook's Hill.

CHAPTER IX

"Valley of Death"

About the time Royall was extricating himself from his predicament, Mills was proceeding with Crook's plan to capture the village. Upon receiving his instructions, Mills formed his three companies below the crest to conceal his motives from the Indians. Trotting down the valley along the left bank, the command quickly was lost from view. Only the crackling sounds of small arms rattling across the countryside broke the stillness of the hot air which now permeated the day.

A low line of hills dominated the left, ending just short of the east bend of the creek. Nearing the bend, a small party of warriors were seen watching the column's approach. Scout Frank Grouard assumed the lead. The command had traveled less than two miles. Approaching the east bend, Captain Alexander Sutorius, with Company E Third Cavalry, was ordered to drive away the warriors watching them from the hilltop. Quickly forming a line, Sutorius drove them from their position "by a bold charge."[1] With this minor obstacle now out the way, the battalion turned north, following the sinewy course of the creek.

Almost as an afterthought, Crook elected to augment Mills' force by detaching and reinforcing the battalion with that of the five companies of the Second Cavalry. Noyes joined Mills shortly after the Sutorious episode. Combined, Mills had at his disposal, eight companies of cavalry consisting of Companies A, E, and M of his own, and five companies of Noyes', Companies A, B, D, E, and I.

A detail of twenty men from Company A, under the direction of Lieutenant Joseph Lawson, was detached to assist the scouts and "keep up connections."[2] To prevent ambush, the column moved parallel, on opposite sides of the creek, with flankers thrown well out. Two miles beyond the east bend, Mills halted to tighten girths and discuss the terrain. At this point, the Rosebud valley tapered to a paltry 150 yards wide. Some of the scouts were becoming restless. Grouard talked to Mills, attempting to persuade the captain not to enter the valley. The scout claimed the canyon was a perfect setting for a trap. As this discussion was taking place, heavy firing could be discerned to the west. Grouard, turning to Mills, declared, "I hear firing in that direction, sir", pointing in the direction of where Crook was known to be.[3]

In a few moments, the command was overtaken by Crook's adjutant, the buckskin clad Azor Nickerson, and his orderly.[4]

"Mills," Nickerson said, "Royall is hard pressed, and must be relieved. Henry is badly wounded and Vroom's troop is all cut up. The General orders that you and Noyes file by your left flank out of this canyon and fall on the rear of the Indians who are pressing Royall."[5]

An astonished Mills doubted the veracity of the directive and asked Nickerson to again repeat the order, and asked, "Are you sure he wants me to go back?"[6]

Nickerson responded that the orders were correct as he had stated.[7] Officers were in disbelief, for many of them thought they were very close to the village. Mills claimed, "We have the village . . . and can hold it."[8]

Orders were orders. There was nothing to do but to adhere to them. Nobody, not even the fiery Mills, would dare circumvent Crook's directive. The column turned left and climbed out of the canyon. Their route came out north of Crook's Hill and to the northeast of Conical Hill. They were now approaching from the rear the warriors seen on Conical Hill who were preparing another sortie toward Crook. The battalion's emergence caught the Indians by surprise and thoroughly disrupted their plans. Spying Mills, the Indians broke off the battle. Some warriors added final insult to injury by making a grand departure. Instead of scattering to the northwest, some warriors elected to ride completely around the army by going down Kollmar Creek to the Rosebud and then riding north down the Rosebud. Mills gave pursuit to the northwest, but it was in vain. Finally, at 2:30 P.M., Mills returned to the main crest. The Battle of the Rosebud was over. It had lasted six hours.

Mills found Crook in the position he had left him. Riding up to the general he asked, "General, why did you recall me? I had the village and could have held it." A dejected Crook gave a melancholy reply,. "Well, Colonel, I found it a more serious engagement than I thought. We have about fifty killed and wounded, and the doctors refused to remain with the wounded unless I left the infantry and one of the squadrons with them. I knew I could not keep my promise to support you with the remainder of the force."[9]

But Crook was not the type of person to give up nor admit he had been beaten. He would try again now that he had his entire command. The day was not over. Still convinced that an Indian village lay down the Rosebud, he organized another strike force. This time he would personally lead it. Leaving his infantry on the crest with the wounded, Crook took his cavalry downstream. Captain Van Vliet and Crawford were positioned as flankers.[10] The scouts assumed the forward advance. Coming to the area where Mills had been overtaken by Nickerson, they halted, refusing to go any further. When asked why the stoppage, the Crows declared the Sioux had laid a trap ahead.[11] An exasperated Crook urged them forward, but the stubborn Crows would not budge. They recounted that in this very spot, a few years before, some of their kin had been massacred by Sioux. They called the area the "Valley of Death."[12] Crook's Indian diplomacy was to no avail. Matters were worsened when Grouard chimed in that he agreed with the scout assessment.[13] Grouard's statement drove the final nails into the coffin. The expedition would have to be aborted from lack of support from the scouts. Crook was not willing to advance without their aid. With deep regret, he turned back, perhaps even believing or wanting to believe that a trap, indeed, lay ahead.

As a matter of fact, Crook had been conned. There was no grand strategem by the Sioux or Crazy Horse to entrap his command in the canyon. Much attention has been made of this entrapment theory. Most notably coming from the pages of histories written by Finerty, Bourke, and Grouard. In the case of Grouard, his biographer embellished on the terrain factor to make the story seem all the more convincing:

> The canyon rose to a height of one thousand feet on both sides of us. The Indians had all of this fortified.[14]

The truth is the canyon is not a steep narrow defile. A survey of the U.S.G.S. map reflects the valley floor averages about 4000 feet, while the commanding bluffs rise to 4400 feet, less than that in other places. This of course makes the ridges 300-400 feet above the canyon. While the valley does taper to 150 feet in the vicinity, it hardly can be characterized as a deep canyon. This impression is easily gained by personal inspection of the area. The lurid writings after the battle have falsified the facts. Finerty labeled the canyon, "a most dangerous defile where all the advantage would be on the side of the savages."[15] Bourke recounted the canyon as "the locality where the savages had planned to entrap the troops, or a large part of them, and wipe them out by closing in upon their rear."[16] General Mills, writing years later, and by now influenced by earlier authors, agreed with the entrapment theory.[17]

The best evidence against the entrapment are the interviews with the Indian participants themselves. Few warriors accounts give credence to the episode. Cheyenne historian George B. Grinnell wrote categorically that the Cheyennes omit any plans of decoy and entrapment.[18] Other historians, such as Father Peter Powell or John Stands In Timber, make no mention of it either.[19] No effort was made by the Indians to trap Mills, for indeed, they did not have inside knowledge that Crook expected the village to be six miles down the valley. No attempt was made by Crazy Horse or any other warrior group to lure the troopers into a deady ambush.[20] Mills' sojourn along the valley floor was unimpeded with the exception of the brushing aside of the small knot of warriors at the east bend. After that, no warriors were ever visible. When Mills filed out of the valley to return to the battlefield, he did so with no hindrance. No Lakota followed in his rear. The entire episode apparently was the excited fantasy of the scouts, with the chief culprit being Frank Grouard.[21]

By 4:00 P.M., Crook returned to the battlefield of the morning. Infantry was posted on Conical Hill until 7:00 P.M. Meanwhile, the balance of the command went into camp in the valley where they had halted before the attack. The wounded were cared for and made as comfortable as possible. Henry was visited by many of the officer corps. Nearly all of them remarked on his pitiful condition for which they could do little. One officer, horrified at the sight of him, remembered his dilemma. A thick blotch of flies had settled on his bandaged face. Henry murmured, "It's all right, Jack, it's what we're here for."[22] Lieutenant Rawolle endeavored to reduce Henry's intense craving for fluids by spoon feeding the captain some red currant jelly rendered soluble by mixing it with water.[23]

Casualties for the six hour fight were low. Ten men killed, including one Indian scout, and 21 soldiers wounded.[24] Exactly how many scouts had been wounded was never reported, or at least not accurately. Crook, in his official report, claimed 13

Indians dead on or in "close proximity of our lines."[25] Crazy Horse calculated their casualties at 39 killed and 63 wounded. This number seems extremely high considering the Plains Indians penchant for not taking many casualties during combat.[26]

Total Sioux and Cheyenne involvement in the battle is estimated at 1000-1500. The Irish pencil-pusher Finerty estimated the soldiers had expended 25,000 rounds of ammunition in the fight.[27] Lieutenant Lemly reported the scouts had fired away 10,000 rounds of ammunition alone. They had been issued 40 rounds per man before leaving Goose Creek.

Crook's dead were presumably "buried where they were killed."[28] Other accounts claim they were "buried at the base of a cut bank along the edge of Rosebud Creek."[29] Noted Indian War historian Walter M. Camp believes they were interred along a side hill.[30]

That evening, Crook held a council. Still persistent that a village lay down the Rosebud, he proposed a night march to find the village and attack it at dawn.[31] His scouts were not impressed with his nocturnal plans. They declined the invitation to participate in the adventure, claiming they were satisfied with the 13 Sioux killed.[32] Perhaps paramout to the Indian decline to go was their shaken faith in the white leader's qualities as a fighter. They had seen nothing during the preceeding battle to impress them.[33] Crook was now totally frustrated. His scouts were balking and talking about returning home. Without their services, Crook was reluctant to do anything, especially advance toward an enemy who had demonstrated an offensive aggressiveness seldom encountered by Plains Indians.

Furthermore, Crook was cognizant that any chance of fully surprising the Lakota had vanished. Even a dawn attack would be at odds. Reluctantly, he decided to withdraw and return to the supply base. There he could replenish his stores, send for reinforcements, and obtain medical attention for his wounded.

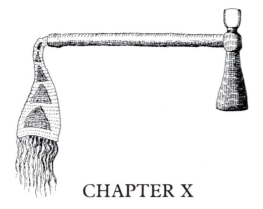

CHAPTER X

Return to Goose Creek

On the 18th, Crook began his return trip to Goose Creek. The wounded were placed in litters, supported between two mules, and in this fashion conveyed over the rough ground.[1] The command had not traveled far before a pathetic sight overcame them. A grievously wounded Sioux was found lying in a ravine near the creek. The unfortunate warrior had been scalped by a Shoshone the day before and left for dead. In addition to the scalping, the victim had been clubbed in the head with vestiges of brain matter protruding through the gaping hole A number of Crows also caught eye of him. They quickly gathered around his frame and chattered excitedly, resembling the discovery of the propinquity of a snake. Showing little humaneness, the Crows attacked him with guns and knives finishing him off in quick and gleeful fashion. In short order, his head and limbs were severed from his body. All that remained was a bloody pulp.[2]

The army's course lay up the south fork of the Rosebud for a few miles following their route of the 17th. In order to circumvent the rough terrain, the route diverted westward in a direction leading them towards the Wolf Mountains. This more circuitous path was taken out of consideration for the wounded in hopes that it would alleviate the jolting. Although the new course would bypass the steep tributaries of the Tongue River drainages, Bourke noted it was not particularly successful. The gains were negated by the innumerable ravines and gullies.[3]

So tedious was the march and so cut up was the terrain, that the unfortunate Henry was dislodged from his mule litter by a sudden movement of one of the mules.[4] The officer tumbled down a twenty foot enbankment, landing on a bed of rocks. White-faced onlookers, after recovering from their shock, scrambled down the earthen ridge to investigte the extent of injuries. Wiping the dirt from his face and lips, they could not get a murmur out of him. Finally, someone brought him water, which cleared out his throat. "How do you feel," amazingly one person queried? The stoic captain replied, "Bully. Never felt better in my life. Everybody is so kind," he continued, and in this tone might have included the "sad-eyed mule which stood innocently winking and blinking near by."[5]

After a grueling 22 miles, camp was pitched near the divide, separating the valleys of the Little Bighorn and Tongue. Before nightfall, the Crows departed for their agency.[6] They informed Crook they would return in 15 days, a vow they never intended to honor. About 1 A.M., nervous pickets opened fire on unknown objects in the darkness. They thought they saw Indians. A reconnaissance was sent out, but failed to disclose any evidence of intruders. Some of the men, their anxiety levels running to full hilt, were overcome by the excitement. They could not return to sleep. Instead, many simply stayed awake, staring into the star-lit night. Others waited for dawn, sipping coffee.[7]

On the 19th, the march was resumed. An uneventful day brought them back to Goose Creek.

General Crook immediately sat down to the task of sending word of his fight to General Sheridan. Crook's telegraphic report written on the 19th was delivered to Sheridan on the 23rd. The two-page report was typical Crook — brief and few of detailed facts. He related the Indians were driven from the field, but he was unable to follow up, owing to the condition of the wounded and running low on provisions.[8] He made no mention that his scouts had abandoned him. The Shoshones left following their return to Goose Creek. Crook further reported he had "ordered five additional companies of Infantry and shall not probably make any extended movement till they arrive."[9]

For the next six weeks the army remained stationary at Goose Creek awaiting reinforcements and additional supplies, and a new body of scouts.

Because of Crook's dilatory action after the battle, some critics have crucified the commander. He has often served as the scapegoat for the disaster that befell Custer eight days later on Little Bighorn. Reporter Davenport was prominent in criticizing Crook's handling of the Rosebud fight. Davenport, who accompanied Royall in the fight, held Crook accountable for the near disaster that almost wiped out Royall.

Colonel Nelson A. Miles, a friend of Custer, and professionally jealous of Crook, also took up the banner that Crook's withdrawal from the field caused the Custer debacle.

Crook was adamant that he had won a hard fought contest, despite attacks by Davenport and others. Writing a report of the battle September 25, 1876, for inclusion in the Report of the Secretary of War Crook declared:

> My troops beat these Indians on a field of their own choosing, and drove them in utter rout from it, as far as the proper care of my wounded and prudence would justify. Subsequent events proved beyond dispute what would have been the fate of the command had the pursuit been continued beyond what judgement dictated.[10]

But Sheridan and others saw through the smokescreen. The facts were plainly visible. Crook had not defeated the Indians or even remotely demoralized them. He may have held the ground, gaining a tactical victory, but he had lost the strategic matchup.[11]

All things considered, it had been an Indian victory. Their objectives had been clearly accomplished — stop Crook before he could reach the village and gain as many war honors as possible. Crook's critics pointed out the realities of the fight; that Crook had been stopped; he had not broken the Indians will to fight; and that he had not pursued with vim and vigor, key elements in waging a successful campaign against nomadic and wandering bands of Indians. Sheridan commented on the Rosebud:

> The victory was barren of results. General Crook was unable to pursue the enemy . . . considering himself too weak to make any movement until additional troops reached him[12]

For years the stigma of defeat on Rosebud Creek haunted Crook's soul. In 1886, he entered heated discussions with Colonel Royall, blaming that officer and Captain Nickerson for the failure of the battle because of their poor conduct.[13] Most of the officer corps supported Crook. Captain Guy Henry denounced the conduct of Royall during the heavy fighting as panicky.[14] A loyal Bourke declared somewhat cryptically that Royall had disobeyed orders and had failed to unite with Crook.[15] Also coming under Crook's wrath was Nickerson. For it was the adjutant, Crook claimed, that had so scattered the troops in the beginning of the battle that allowed for the poor showing of the command. Privately, Crook termed Royall "an ingrate, treacherous, and cowardly to boot."[16] Captain Mills, who appears to have always spoken his mind, said that "Crook ought to have shot some officers."[17] Excepting Davenport, the reporters as a whole were unanimously favorable to Crook.

Davenport reported in the *New York Herald* that Crook's retreat left Sitting Bull free to "choose the future seat of his operations."[18] The *Herald* renewed its unceasing diatribes, charging Crook with mismanaging the campaign. "Crook won no laurels as the commander of the expedition against the Indians. The battle was a surprise, and one thing which the whole history of Indian warfare proves that, it is the supreme duty of a commander to guard against surprise."[19] The *Herald* finished its long tirade by denouncing "If General Crook is to serve further against the Indians it should be in a subordinate capacity."[20]

The Battle of the Rosebud will never match the Little Bighorn for sheer dramatic intensity, nor is it assessed with the degree of controversy rivaling that affair. Yet, because of its relation to that fight, it has found itself centered in debate, speculation, and controversy. The Rosebud has fueled both Crook defenders and detractors. The responsibility for the outcome of the battle and the great number of "what ifs" have insured its rightful place in history. No satisfactory answers will be discovered to everyone's liking, however, the following statements seem to be accurate:

(1) The military from the Commander of the Army on down to the lowliest private seemed to have grossly underestimated the fighting qualities of the Sioux and Cheyenne. No one expected the Indians to concentrate their forces in one place for such a large attack.

(2) The Indians fought more as a compact unit, reflecting cohesion and organization, seldom encountered in Indian war fighting. The soldiers were caught off guard by this unusual display of conventional warfare. After adjusting to organized attacks, the Indians shifted back into guerrilla-style tactics, which totally frustrated and disrupted the rhythm of the army.

(3) Crook committed the unpardonable sin of being caught napping. Cognizant that he was in enemy territory, he failed to execute rudimentary procedures. He did not post adequate pickets as a precaution against surprise attacks. Crook's lackadaisical attitude of allowing his men to unsaddle and rest their horses when he had been warned that Indians were in the area, is inexcusable. The entire campaign took on the appearance of a summer's long picnic.

(4) Crook was overconfident, a disease he shared with his officers. The concern was not so much in fighting the Indians as much as it was in trying to maneuver them back to the reservations.

(5) The command became too widely scattered after the initial Indian assault. Crook, in later years, and with some validity, held Captain Nickerson and Lieutenant Colonel Royall responsible. Both officers seemed to have deployed the command and in the process scattered it over a wide area. The piecemeal attacks that followed returned no beneficial gain.

(6) The scattering of the cavalry to the west was due to the efforts of Royall. Without informing Crook of his intentions, he dashed off on a fruitless venture, that in affect, reduced Crook's cavalry force by one-third. Royall's action also placed him well beyond any support from Crook.

(7) Royall became embroiled in a battle that he could not easily terminate. The sending of Meinhold to Crook was a serious mistake on two counts. First, it reduced Royall's stength by 20%. Second, the transferring of Meinhold clearly demonstrated that if Royall would have taken the entire command at once, he could have probably gotten through unscathed.

(8) Crook's decision to send over half his cavalry to find and hold a phantom village opened the gates for the Indians to press their attacks, particularly against the reduced force of Royall.

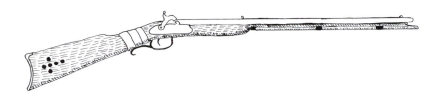

CHAPTER XI

Crook and the Custer Connection

The Battle of the Rosebud by Indian War standards was a behemoth confrontation. It represents an atypical encounter on the Western frontier because large masses of troops rarely clashed with extensive Indian forces. The Rosebud was overshadowed, and rightfully so, by the stunning and shocking defeat on Little Bighorn, June 25. Army officers, journalists, and civilians asked the same questions, how could it happen? Accordingly, some people blamed the Custer tragedy on General George Crook. An article in the *Army-Navy Journal* dated July 6, was one of the first to place Custer's demise in the lap of Crook. Crook was censored on two counts, first for not taking his provisions with him, which made follow up pursuit impractical, and second, for not striking out from Goose Creek shortly after he returned.

The extremely vitriolic and blatantly ambitious Nelson Miles assumed the banner of protecting Custer. Miles openly criticized Terry and Crook for which he had little respect. Miles, in an August 2, 1876, letter to his wife, wrote, "from all I can learn from the officers, General Crook makes no comments or gives General Terry any information. I think it almost a military crime that these two commands are not under one head and governed by the simplest principles of war."[1] Miles considered Crook vacillatory and unreliable.

Crook had his supporters, too. One of the most powerful and

most influential being General of the Army, William T. Sherman. Sherman thought highly of Crook's military skills. He considered him foremost of his western Indian commanders. Despite Sherman's favorable impression of Crook, he was not above calling a spade a spade. He severely criticized Crook for not exerting pressure on the Sioux before and after the Rosebud fight. Moreover, Sherman was annoyed by the multitude of journalists covering Crook's campaign. Sherman, who had come to disdain the press, was chagrined that Crook received widespread notoriety, while the efforts of Terry's command received scant mention.[2]

In all fairness to Crook, he can not be held accountable for Custer's shortcomings at Little Bighorn. Contemporary historians and devout admirers of Custer have been blinded by the basic facts of the campaign. At the root of their contention is that Crook was negligent in not informing either Terry or Custer of his battle and thereby warning them of the great masses and fighting savvy they would be up against. It is senseless to have expected Crook to have sent a courier to either officer. He had only a vague idea where they were supposed to be — somewhere to the northeast, marching below the Yellowstone. The information on Gibbon was outdated and incomplete. When Grouard returned with the Crow delegation of scouts on June 14, Gibbon was reported to be at the mouth of the Tongue or Rosebud, a hundred miles away. How was Crook to get a courier through with news of the battle? None of the scouts would have risked such a venture, knowing full well that an extensive number of Lakota were between them and Gibbon. Following the Custer disaster, Terry was faced with the identical problem. It was not until July 12, 15 days after the Custer fight, that Terry succeeded in getting a messenger through to Crook. That endeavor succeeded only after an earlier failure because of fear of Indians in the vicinity.

Arriving on Goose Creek, June 19, Crook did forward a

telegraphic message to Sheridan, describing his engagement. He cannot be accused of not warning his superiors.[3]

We can reverse the tables on this scenario. When Terry, Custer, Gibbon, and Brisbin met aboard the *Far West*, June 21, they charted out their strategy. Suffice it to say, their plans of enveloping the warriors does not include any cooperation with Crook. And there was good reason for not incorporating Crook into the operation. They did not know his position, nor Crook theirs. Both commands, actually independent departmental commands, were operating independently of the other. One must remember and take council that Terry and Crook were separate commanders. Their primary focus of consideration was the affairs immediately within their jurisdiction. Sheridan's overall strategy called for a three-prong campaign, but it was not neccessarily expected that the two departments would act in close concert, considering the vast expanse of territory to recon-noitor. And of most importance in evaluating the cooperation or lack of cooperation between the commanders, is the movement of the Indians. The migratory patterning of the Indians would dictate the army's movement. The very foundation of the cam-paign was built on a presumption that if the Lakota avoided contact with one column, that the other command would be in a position to crush Indian resistance, or at the very least, maneuver the bands eastward toward the reservations.

Critics of Crook charge him with dilatory action bordering on apathy towards the other column, following the Rosebud fight. Crook returned to his supply base to pass away valuable time, fishing and big game hunting. They accuse him of not being aggressive in the face of the Indians. These charges are undenia-ble and can hardly be defended. Crook's complacency in camp while waiting further men and supplies does nothing for his already tarnished reputation. Those accusations, to an extent, are justifiable, but they do not reflect the entire picture. Supplies were running low. He did not have the advantage that Terry and

Gibbon enjoyed. Terry's troops were easily supplied, having the advantage of steamboats to drop off provisions and equipment along the banks of the Yellowstone. Crook had to depend on a costly and laborious land route of 175 miles connecting Fort Fetterman to Goose Creek to keep his men in the field. The aftermath of Rosebud convinced Crook he needed troop reinforcements and additional supplies to sustain himelf in the field. Because of the distance involved, it would require six weeks to adequately resupply and reinforce his Army. True, the command did enjoy the spartan luxury of basking in the shadows of the Big Horn Mountains, enjoying the amenities of hunting and fishing. Hunting and fishing expeditions were encouraged. They provided an outlet to the dull and monotonous routines of camp life. By themselves, there was nothing wrong with this type of exercise.

Proponents of Custer have often stated, had the enegetic Custer or someone else possessing more vigor been at the helm of Crook's column, the battle of the Rosebud would have ended differently. Perhaps so. The same logic, if applied to Custer at Little Bighorn, dictates that affiairs there may have ended differently, too. It is to Crook's credit that he fought the Battle of the Rosebud as a field commander. Custer fought the Battle of the Little Bighorn as if he was a line officer, rather than a regimental commander. Shortly after the fighting on the Rosebud broke out, Crook assumed control. He quickly went to the high ground where he could superintend overall operations and perceive changing developments in the battle. He made an error in judgement by sending Mills down the Rosebud in what turned out as the pivotal move in the entire fight. But at least, he did not join his senior captain in the sortie and as a result lose total visual contact of the actions on the other portion of the field. Crook's presence on the ground allowed him to divert troops to support Royall in his time of need and accurately recall Mills when the battle shifted in favor of the Indians. The unfortunate Custer demonstrated at Little Bighorn one of his biggest weaknesses. Mainly, his penchant for acting more like a line or battalion commander rather than a regimental commander. Custer lost visual contact with Reno and became hopelessly ignorant of affairs other than those in his immediate front. Lack of communiations between Custer and his fragmented battalions doomed him to failure and death. The erstwhile Crook conducted a poorly fought battle at Rosebud, but he did not become a tragic victim like Custer, only a scapegoat for Custer's demise.

Terrain

Crook's camp on morning of June 17. Van Vliet Hill in background, looking west.

Marker on Crook's Hill; Van Vliet Hill in background, looking south.

Conical Hill, bastion of Indian defense.

Bluffs taken by Capt. Mills' in his first charge. Indians utilized the pine-studded slopes and large boulders for defense.

Kollmar Creek. Taken from Crook's Hill looking north.

Marker noting Royall's third position and scene of most bloody fighting during Battle of the Rosebud.

Slab of rock marks the approximate location where Henry was wounded.

Crook's Hill as seen from Royall's third position. Wooded area in center denotes led horse ravine, view looking north; Burt and Burrowes Ridge is to the extreme right of photo.

Burt and Burrows Ridge. Upper center with white banks showing.

"Canyon of the Rosebud," view looking north.

Mills Canyon. Taken at point where he returned to battlefield from Conical Hill.

Principals

A Brady photograph shows Sheridan and four of his chief architects of the Shenandoah Valley Campaign 1864-65. All of them would turn Civil War investments into profitable careers as Indian Fighters. General Crook is seated center. Crook was at the zenith of his military career in the early days of the 1864 offensive. He suffered a self-imposed fallout with his superior, Sheridan, over the Battle of Cedar Creek in October, 1864. Left to right are Wesley Merritt, Philip Sheridan, George Crook, James W. Forsyth, and George A. Custer.

GENERAL GEORGE CROOK

Dressed resplendently in a regulation uniform, Crook habitually shunned conformity on the campaign. His usual habiliments consisted of a private's overcoat or a canvas hunting suit. At the outset of the 1876 Sioux War, Crook basked in the glory of being the public's personification of an Indian fighter. Outwardly, he demonstrated little of the shameless self-aggrandizing that characterized Nelson Miles and George Custer, yet, inwardly, the calculating Crook wore a rowel of ambition as sharp as anyone in the Army. Bitter professional jealousies with Sheridan and Terry hindered full-scale cooperation in 1876 and prompted outsiders to point fingers at Crook as the responsible agent for Custer's demise.

Courtesy Custer Battlefield National Monument.

COLONEL JOSEPH J. REYNOLDS Patriarch of the Third Cavalry, Reynolds grasped defeat from the jaws of victory on Powder River. His ineptness so incurred the wrath of Crook that he was court-martialed and found guilty of mismanaging the campaign. Sentenced to a one year suspension, Reynolds never recovered from the stigma attached to the affair, and he retired in June, 1877. Reynolds' trial produced bitter recriminations between Crook and officers of the Third. Courtesy Custer Battlefield National Monument

CAPTAIN HENRY NOYES From the West Point class of 1861, this Maine native spent the entire Civil War in the Second Cavalry. By war's end he had earned a Major's brevet. His lackluster performance on Powder River tarnished his reputation, but not to the point of relieving him of command responsibility. In charge of the Second Cavalry battalion at Rosebud, he performed well. Overshadowed by the Third Cavalry, his battalion played but a minor role in the fighting. Dignified in appearance, he was not disposed to pick quarrels with officers of the Third.

FRANK GROUARD

Standing six feet tall and weighing in excess of two hundred pounds, the swarthy complexioned Grouard presented an imposing sight. Crook was duly impressed with his scouting abilities, for Grouard, like few other men in the region, knew the peculiarities of the Sioux, having lived so long amongst them. He manifested an air of credibility and seemingly persuasive powers to boot. Almost single-handedly he convinced Crook that to continue down Rosebud "canyon" would invite impending disaster for his troops, a prophecy that was not based on a bed of firm evidence. Grouard's assertion that a sizeable warrior force lay in ambush was put to good use by Crook who used the statements to help justify his return to Goose Creek.

Courtesy Custer Battlefield, Camp Collection.

LT. JOHN BOURKE
Perhaps no commanding general ever had a more devout and faithful aide than Crook had in John G. Bourke. Possessing intellectual capacity far superior to his peers, Bourke's career shadowed his mentor Crook. It is largely through Bourke's penchant for details and his prolific note taking that many incidences of the expedition are preserved.
Courtesy Custer Battlefield National Monument

LT. THADDEUS CAPRON
Sporting mutton chops liken to General Ambrose Burnside of Civil War fame, Capron played but a subordinate role in the Rosebud affair as second in command of Company C 9th Infantry. The checkmate on the Rosebud was nothing compared to the personal tragedy Capron suffered when he learned on June 22 that his two-year old son, Henry, had suddenly died.
Courtesy Fort Laramie National Historic Site.

PLENTY COUPS

Typical of the scouts who served with Crook on the Rosebud is Plenty Coups. Vibrant and youthful, he operated not out of admiration for the bluecoats, but more for the opportunity of retribution against his Tribe's nemesis, the Sioux and Cheyenne. Rosebud would earn him war honors, later to be put to use in leading his Nation's fight for equality and respect in the white man's world.

Courtesy Custer Battlefield National Monument.

LITTLE BIG MAN

Cousin and rival of Crazy Horse, Little Big Man exemplifies the fighting qualities of the Oglala Sioux at Rosebud. Never given the acclaim accorded others like Crazy Horse, he represents the spirit and tenacity of the Sioux, hoping to retain their cultural way of life on the Plains. Lt. Bourke, who became acquainted with Little Big Man, considered him "a man of considerable ability and force."

Courtesy of Custer Battlefield National Monument.

MAJOR ALEXANDER CHAMBERS
A West Point classmate of
George Crook, he assembled
an enviable record during the
Civil War. Solid and
dependable, he possessed both
administrative and combat
skills. Although his mule
brigade brought out a chorus
of laughters from the enlisted
cavalrymen, his battalion of
mule riders more than proved
their mettle at Rosebud. Close
at hand with Crook during the
fighting, he was not afforded
an opportunity to demonstrate
his ability to handle
independent command.
Courtesy Fort Laramie National
Historic Site.

LIMPY
This Cheyenne was so named
because a birth defect left him
with one leg shorter than the
other. His handicap did not
prevent him from taking part in
the Battle of the Rosebud or the
Little Bighorn. At the Rosebud,
he was knocked from his horse,
but managed to climb on some
rocks and leap behind Young Two
Moon before soldiers could draw
a bead on him.
Courtesy Custer Battlefield National
Monument.

GUY V. HENRY

A West Pointer like his father, Henry emerged from the Civil War with a Colonel's brevet. Frail health and a cadaverous appearance did nothing to dampen his ardor. Unflinching in combat, he handled his troops at the Rosebud with the precision of a drillmaster. His horrible wounding at the height of battle signalled the turning point in the contest. Despite his painful injury, Henry's stoicism further endeared support from his admiring companions.

Courtesy Wyoming State Archives and Historical Department.

Two Moon

Best known for his exploits in the Little Bighorn fight, Two Moon also saw action at Rosebud. Never a large tribe, compared to the Sioux, the Cheyennes, like Two Moon, allied with their friends in contesting continual encroachment upon their lands.

ANDREW S. BURT

Son of a prosperous Cincinnati banker, Burt left Yale in his junior year. Joining a volunteer regiment from Ohio, he soon illustrated military capabilities despite his formal lack of training. Brevets were awarded for meritorious conduct at Mill Springs, Kentucky; Atlanta Campaign and Jonesboro, Georgia. In 1866, he found himself on the remote frontier, serving in the 18th Infantry. Here he served for the better part of his career. Small in stature, his twinkling grey eyes cast a countenance towards the spur of duty. At Rosebud, he capitalized on opportunity. He was at the right place at the right time.

ANSON MILLS

Savant he was not, having been discharged from West Point after two and one-half years. Ambitious and successful he was. The outbreak of the Civil War found him with an antedated commission in the Regular Army. Promotions and brevets through the rank of Lieutenant Colonel followed. He was handsome with jet black hair, piercing dark eyes, and a goatee trimmed in the style of the period. In speech he was abrupt and easily excitable. Mills was quick to criticize, as evidenced by his disparaging remarks following the Powder River and Rosebud. Crook stored supreme confidence in his adroitness by assigning him tasks far beyond his rank throughout the campaign. At Rosebud, he was ordered to strike and hold a phantom village. Only his untimely recall prevented him from discovering the truth; that no village existed and indeed, that no large contending warrior element waited in concealment to annihilate his force. Mills obeyed his directive and returned to the battlefield like the professional soldier he was.

MARKERS ON ROSEBUD BATTLEFIELD

Nine lonely markers stood mute overlooking the battlefield on Rosebud Creek when this photograph was taken by noted Cheyenne historian Dr. Thomas B. Marquis September 6, 1925. Controversy surrounds the exact burial site for the men killed in the battle. Conflicting accounts claim the dead were buried along the bank of the creek. Still others maintain the deceased were placed in a side ravine. Medical Director for the Expedition, Albert Hartsuff, wrote in his report that "all the dead were buried where they were killed." The markers in this picture are symbolic gestures only. They were placed on a hilltop near the east bend of the Rosebud. They seemingly were cannibalized by local ranchers as weights for plows or other utilitarian functions.

Courtesy Custer Battlefield National Monument.

Maps

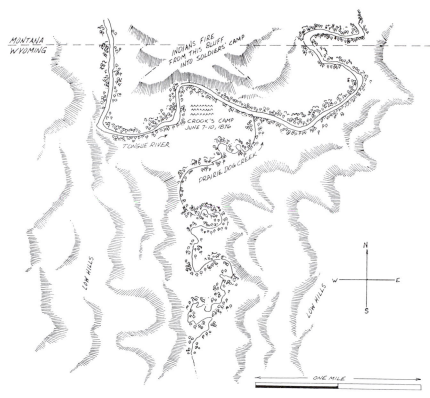

CROOK'S FIGHT ON THE PRAIRIE DOG, JUNE 9, 1876

Map drawn by George Mathews

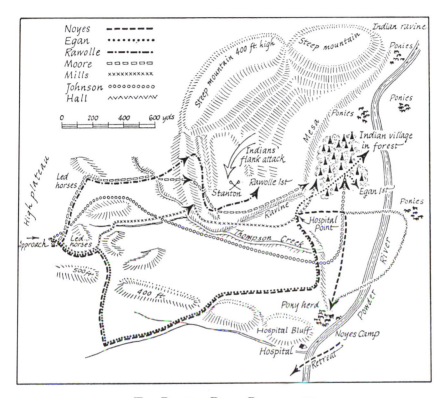

THE POWDER RIVER BATTLEFIELD

The Powder River Battlefield, March 17, 1876. Reprinted from J.W. Vaughn, *The Reynolds Campaign on Powder River* (Norman: University of Oklahoma Press, 1961). Reprinted with permission.

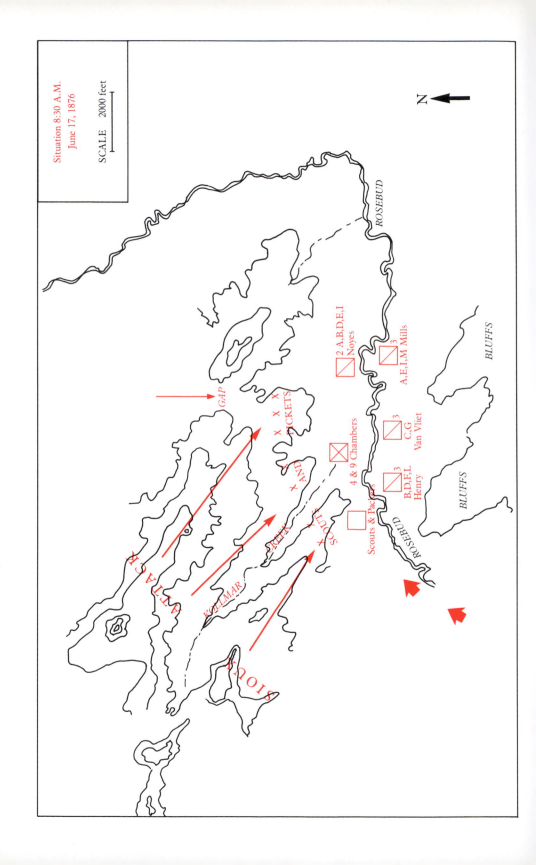

Situation 8:30 A.M.
June 17, 1876

SCALE   2000 feet

N

ROSEBUD

BLUFFS

BLUFFS

2 A,B,D,E,I
Noyes

3
A,E,I,M Mills

3
C,G
Van Vliet

4 & 9 Chambers

3
B,D,F,L
Henry

X X X
X X
X PICKETS

X AND

X SCOUTS

Scouts & Packers

GAP

ATTACK

KOLLMAR

SIOUX

ROSEBUD

Situation 8:30 a.m.

Warriors converge on Crook from the north and northwest. Crow and Shoshone scouts skirmish with attackers providing the surprised soldiers time to recover from the initial assault.

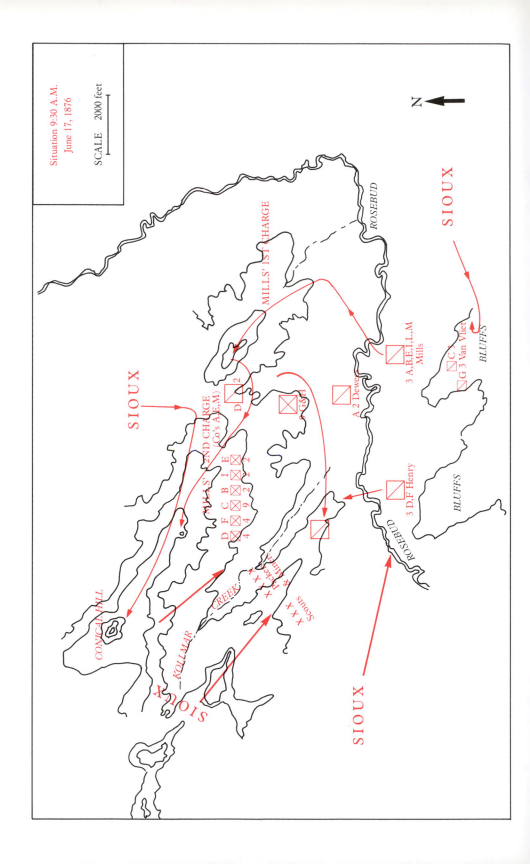

Situation 9:30 A.M.
June 17, 1876

SCALE   2000 feet

N

SIOUX

SIOUX

SIOUX

SIOUX

SIOUX

ROSEBUD

BLUFFS

BLUFFS

BLUFFS

ROSEBUD

MILLS' 1ST CHARGE

MILLS' 2ND CHARGE
(Co's A,E,M)

CONICAL HILL

KOLLMAR

CREEK

Scouts
& Inftry.

3 A,B,E,I,L,M
Mills

C,
G 3 Van Vliet

A 2 Dewees

3 D,F Henry

D   2

8 H

D F C B I E
4 4 9 2 2 2

Indian attack spreads east and west north of camp. Van Vliet's battalion is sent south of creek to high bluffs. He reaches the top in time to turn back Sioux thrust attempting to take the same heights from the east. Captain Henry's two companies are posted upstream from camp to block Indians from advancing down the creek from the west. Major Chambers and infantry move northward as skirmishers supported by the dismounted battalion of Second Cavalry under Captain Noyes. Captain Mills leads six companies of cavalry on his first charge which succeeds in driving Sioux and Cheyenne from their defensive position east of gap. Mills reforms his command and with three companies drives the warriors from Crook's Hill to Conical Hill.

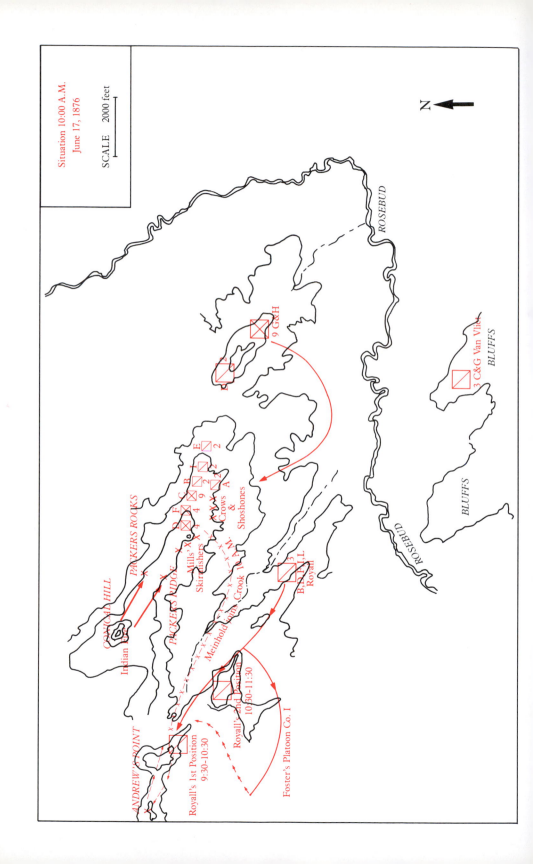

N

ROSEBUD

9 G&H
E

3 C&G Van Vliet
BLUFFS

BLUFFS

ROSEBUD

E 2
B 2
C 9
D 4
F 4
A
Crows & Shoshones

PACKERS ROCKS

CONICAL HILL

Indian

PACKERS RIDGE

Mills' X
Skirmishers X
Meinhold join Crook 10:45
M
F
3
B, D, I, L
Royall

Royall's 2nd Position
10:30-11:30

ANDREW' POINT

Royall's 1st Position
9:30-10:30

Foster's Platoon Co. I

SITUATION 10:00 A.M.

On the center and right warriors melt in the face of Crook's general advance. Crook establishes headquarters on Crook's Hill. From here a desultory fire is maintained with Indians on Conical Hill. Colonel Royall on the extreme left has advanced one mile beyond Crook's left. He halts at first position at head of Kollmar Creek. Crook sends a messenger to Royall requesting he return. Instead of returning Royall sends the solitary company of Meinhold. Warriors begin to concentrate on Royall's isolated column.

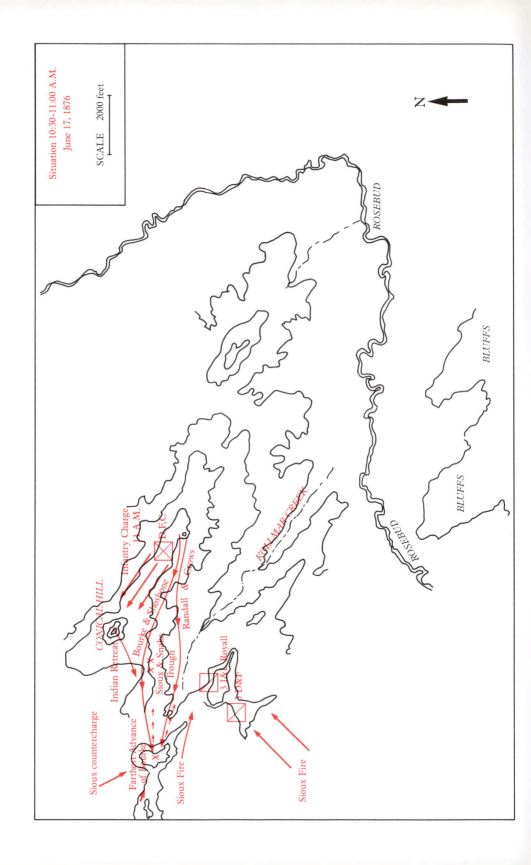

Situation 10:30–11:00 A.M.
June 17, 1876

SCALE   2000 feet

N

ROSEBUD

BLUFFS

BLUFFS

BLUFFS

ROSEBUD

KOLLMAR CREEK

CONICAL HILL

Infantry Charge
11 A.M.

E, C

Bourke & Shoshone

Randall & Crows

Indian Retreat

Sioux & Snake
Trough

Sioux countercharge

Farthest Advance
of Horses

X

Sioux Fire

3 I & Royall

D & F

Sioux Fire

Sioux Fire

Indians streaming back from their sortie down Kollmar are met by the Crow and Shoshone under Randall and Bourke. Scouts drive into the flanks of the warriors forcing them west to a point beyond Royall's first position. Around 11 A.M. infantry from Crook's Hill advance in skirmish line formation toward Conical Hill. Warriors are unable to withstand the attack and retreat. On the extreme left Royall continues to fend off Indian assaults from the high ground at his second position.

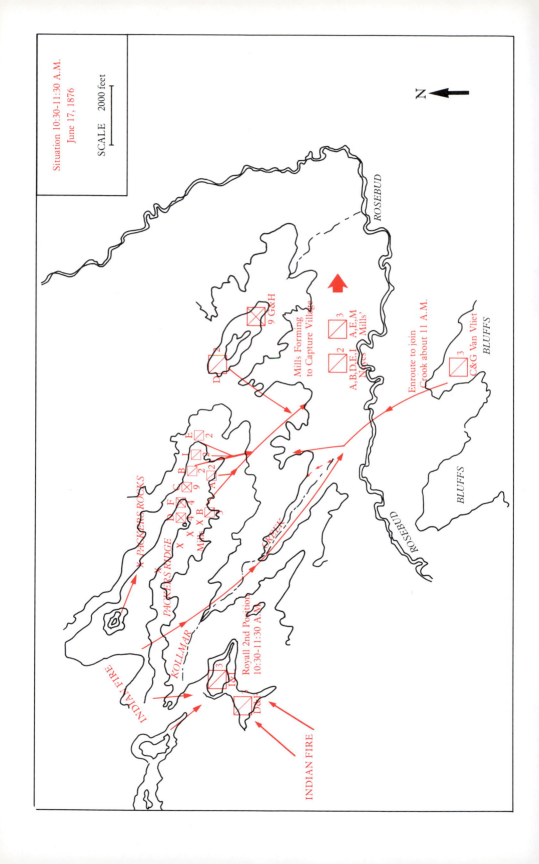

Situation 10:30–11:30 A.M.
June 17, 1876

SCALE   2000 feet

N

ROSEBUD

9 G&H

D 2

Mills Forming
to Capture Village

3
A,E,M
Mills'

2
A,B,D,E,I,
Noyes

Enroute to join
Crook about 11 A.M.

BLUFFS

3
C&G Van Vliet

BLUFFS

ROSEBUD

E 2

C B 2

F C B 2
9

A 2

D F E
4

W X B
X

PACKER'S ROCKS

PACKER'S RIDGE

KOLLMAR

Royall 2nd Position
10:30–11:30 A.M.

3
I

D,F

INDIAN FIRE

INDIAN FIRE

SITUATION 10:30-11:30 A.M.

Believing the Sioux could only be fighting so fiercely out of protection for their village, Crook detaches Mills and Noyes with orders to attack and hold the village suspected of being just down the Rosebud. Meanwhile Crook would hold the balance of his command and wait for Royall to return before following Mills. Warriors raid down Kollmar Creek to its mouth. Van Vliet checks their progress. On the left Royall is coming under increasingly heavy assualts. He retreats south to his second position.

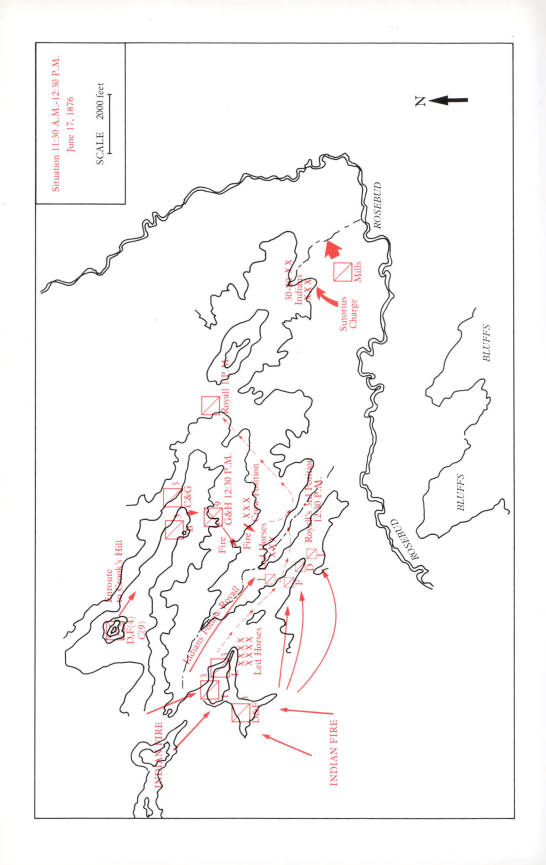

Situation 11:30 A.M.–12:30 P.M.
June 17, 1876

SCALE   2000 feet

N

ROSEBUD

ROSEBUD

BLUFFS

BLUFFS

BLUFFS

30–40
Indians
XXX

Sutorius
Charge

Mills

Royall 1P.M.

C&G

3

Fire G&H 12:30 P.M.

Fire XXX
Troop Attrition

Led Horses
XXX

Royall's 3rd Position
12:30 P.M.

D
T
F
I

Enroute
to Crook's Hill

D,F(4)
C(9)

Indians Follow Royall

XXX
XXXX
Led Horses

3

INDIAN FIRE

INDIAN FIRE

SITUATION 11:30 A.M.–12:30 P.M.

At 11:30 A.M. Royall initiates a mile-long retrograde movement along the ridge top. Warriors follow on flanks and rear preventing the cavalry from making a run to join Crook. At a position directly south of Crook's Hill and separated from Crook by Kollmar Creek, Royall makes his stand. He prepares to mount his men and make dash to unite with Crook. It is too late. Warriors converge on his command at his third position. Captain Vroom's company is badly cut up. Captain Guy V. Henry is grievously wounded. Crook, seeing their predicament, dispatches infantry companies of Burt and Burrowes and scouts to extricate Royall. On the right Mills brushes past a small knot of Sioux near the east bend and begins his advance down the Rosebud to locate the village.

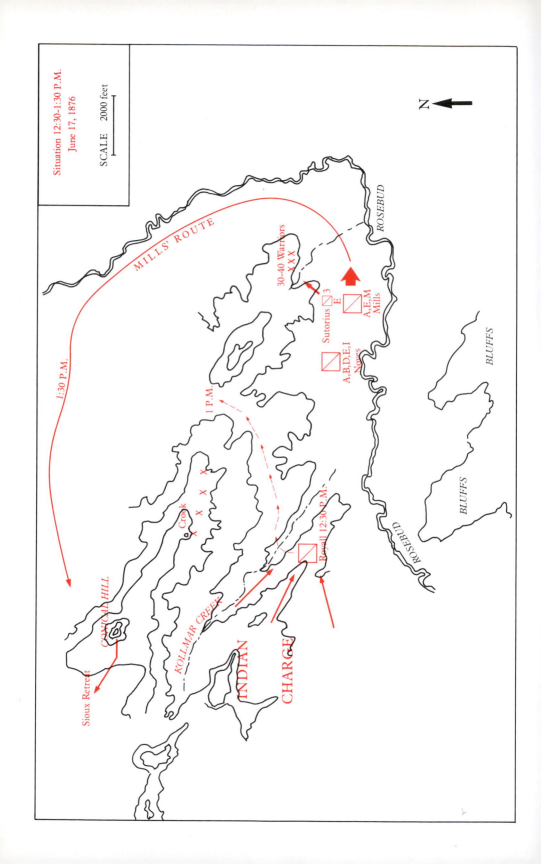

Situation 12:30-1:30 P.M.
June 17, 1876

SCALE   2000 feet

N

MILLS' ROUTE

1:30 P.M.

ROSEBUD

30-40 Warriors
X X X

Sutorius 3
E

A,E,M
Mills

A,B,D,E,I
Noyes

BLUFFS

1 P.M.

BLUFFS

Crook
X X X

Royall 12:30 P.M.

ROSEBUD

CONICAL HILL

KOLLMAR CREEK

Sioux Retreat

INDIAN

CHARGE

With the aid of infantry and scouts attack on Royall is repulsed but not without severe casualties for Indian war fighting. Around 1 P.M. Royall mounts his men and passes east of Burt and Burrowes. He places his men on line near the gap. Crook at 12:30 p.m. sends aide Nickerson to Mills with orders to return to the battlefield. Mills defiles from the valley and onto the rear of Indians massing for another attack from Conical Hill. Mills' approach scatters the Indians ending the six hour struggle.

CHAPTER XII
Epilogue

General Crook would visit Rosebud Battlefield one more time. On August 7, 1876, his column camped north of the site. This time he would not be surprised and he would have additional troops to throw at the Indians should they become bold and daring. Crook's camp in August was doubled in size reaching 2500 men. There was no surprise attack. The Indians had scattered, following the Little Bighorn. The punishing stern chase of late summer had begun in earnest for Terry and Crook. Their commands finally formed a junction on the Rosebud, August 10. The columns stayed united, but only for a brief span. They eventually spilt up, each going their separate way.

Tenacity was always a hallmark of Crook, even if it was punctuated with erratic results. While Powder River and Rosebud had done nothing to embellish his reputation, a small victory at Slim Buttes, September 9 and 10, did produce a settling effect and restore confidence in the troops. Crook followed up the Slim Buttes fight with a winter campaign in the Powder River country of north-central Wyoming. Crook unleashed the extremely efficient and capable Ranald S. Mackenzie. Mackenzie led a successful foray in late November on Dull Knife's Cheyennes on a tributary of the Powder River near present day Kaycee, Wyoming. Slim Buttes and Dull Knife neutralized the poor showing at Rosebud, but they could not entirely replace the stigma attached to it, particularly in the light following Custer's annihilation.

In a short span, the Rosebud was all but forgotten. The defeat of Custer relegated Crook's battle to secondary importance. Since Indian War battles were primarily skirmishes in the first place, secondary importance meant that it was to be nearly forgotten. With each passing generation, the Rosebud was remembered by fewer individuals. The accounts of Bourke and Finerty kept the battle from drifting off into total obscurity. Occasionally, the battle was given scant notice in a Custer fight publication, usually in the form of a passing footnote.

The battlefield itself was unmarked and abandoned. Within a decade after the battle, Euro-Americans supplanted the Indians in the region. Cattle raising became the chief economic enterprise on Rosebud Battlefield.

Walter M. Camp, editor of the *Railroad Review,* and a devout student of the Indian Wars, was instrumental in identifying and promoting the site. In 1920, Camp had placed on the battlefield nine marble markers to memorialize and pay homage to the American soldiers killed in combat during the battle.[1]

Interest in the Rosebud fight never obtained mammoth proportions, but it did nourish and foster a small crowd of followers. One such person was a local rancher, Slim Kobold, who owned much of the land encompassing the battlefield. Through the efforts of Mr. Kobold and a few others, the battlefield was officially dedicated in 1934. A monument was placed at the east bend of the Rosebud on top of a small knoll where Camp had his markers erected 14 years earlier. A throng of 1000 or more spectators was on hand for the unveiling done under the auspices of the Billings Chapter of the Shining Mountain Chapter Daughters of the American Revolution. Four aged Cheyenne veterans of the battle, Louis Dog, Limpy, Weasel Bear, and Bear Heart attended the ceremonies.[2] But concern for the site remained minimal. Not until the 1950s did anyone take a serious view of the battle. Windsor, Colorado, lawyer Jesse W. Vaughn, began making repeated trips to the battleground. He also brought along a metal detector. Vaughn delved into the battle using his metal detector as an instrument to identify the metallic cartridges which outlined the soldier-Indian positions. Kobold assisted Vaughn in his undertaking. They formed a common friendship, fostered around the battle. Vaughn's field trips consumed years, but resulted in an accurate reconstruction of most of the battlefield's major areas. In 1956, Vaughn published his work on the battle of the Rosebud, *With Crook at the Rosebud*. While Vaughn's efforts spurred additional visitors, perhaps an additional hundred or so, it did nothing to preserve the battlefield itself.

It took the visionary efforts of landowner Slim Kobold, the battlefield's most ardent supporter, to find a means to preserve the site. Kobold went about marking the field. He and Miles City archeologist, Joe Dent, erected small concrete pyramids at key positions. Kobold and Dent placed their markers in 1961.

The Rosebud battlefield underwent its biggest fight in the 1970s. Coal, millions of tons of "black gold," lay just beneath the surface of the ground. Kobold could have easily sold his ranch to mining developers, however, Kobold the preservationist, had another plan. He became the chief architect in preserving the battlefield. Kobold began an unending vigil of letter writing to state and national dignataries in an all-out attempt to preserve the Rosebud. His efforts paid huge dividends when in 1972, the Rosebud Battlefield was placed on the National Register of Historic Places. In 1976, the centennial year of the Battle of the Rosebud, Slim's dream of preserving the battlefield became reality when the State of Montana purchased the land.

While Kobold was winning his preservation struggles, he was losing a personal battle. Dying of cancer, Kobold, from his hospital bed in Billings, signed the papers in 1978, making Rosebud Battlefield a state monument.

Today the site is under development. A series of metal inter-
pretive panels at the park's entrance gives visitors an overview of
the battle. The future is bright for the park. State officials will
begin work on a general management plan. Aesthetically, the site
of the battlefield is one of unsurpassed beauty. The battlefield
has not been a victim of overdevelopment. Visitors can walk
over the ground and ponder the movements of both warriors and
soldiers. There is little in the way of man-made creations to
blemish the landscape. Without a doubt, the Rosebud Battlefield
occupies one of the loveliest settings of any battlefield in the
United States. A visit to the park will gain one a sense of what it
must have been like to have fought in the battle.

Unlike the Custer Battlefield, which has 300,000 visitors a
year, the Rosebud is visited by only a token few who have
studied the fight and know of its importance and existence. Even
those students, the most ardent of Indian War battle enthusiats,
must make a special effort to travel to the place. The battlefield is
accessible only by a scoria-based road leading north from Decker,
Montana, or from a combination paved-graveled road leading
south from Busby, Montana. The Battle of the Rosebud will
always be overshadowed by the tragedy at Little Bighorn, but it
has awakened interest to grab its rightful place in history as
an important episode in the conflict of cultures which dominated
the western frontier in the period immediately following the
Civil War.

Appendices, Notes, Bibliography
and Index

Appendices

Appendix A
COMPANY ROSTERS OF OFFICERS AND MEN AT BATTLE OF ROSEBUD
JUNE 17, 1876

The following officers and men served in the Battle of the Rosebud. Their names were taken off Company Muster rolls for the period ending June 30, 1876. Those officers and men who did not serve in the campaign are omitted. To avoid confusion, the names of the men killed are listed on the rolls here even though they were removed from the June 30 roll. Soldiers killed in action are marked (*) beside their name. If a soldier was wounded in the battle the symbol (†) will appear beside his name. The following roster was taken from the National Archives and first compiled by J. W. Vaughn as an appendix in his work *With Crook at the Rosebud*.

Fourth Infantry D Company

CAPTAIN
Avery B. Cain
FIRST LIEUTENANT
Henry Seton
FIRST SARGEANT
Reichert Z. Dexter
SARGEANT
Smith Chittenen
John F. Cochrane
Bernard Degnan
Joseph Lister
CORPORAL
Thomas Conley

Alfred F. Funk
TRUMPETER
James Connelly
Alfred Smith
ARTIFICER
Charles McMahon
PRIVATE
John Benazet
Charles R. Bill
John H. Bishop
George W. Bowley
Carl Dahlman

Peter Decker
†James Devine
James Devlin
David F. Dowling
John Edwards
Louis Eiskamp
†Richard Flynn
Phillip George
John Hall
Richard Haney
Irving Heaslip
Patrick Higerty

Leon Lawrence
Gilbert Long
Thomas Maher
Daniel McCormick
Ezekial Morgan
William Perry
Lawrence Schneiderhan
Joshua Scott
Charles Stollnow
†John H. Terry
Albert Wagner
Edward Williams

Fourth Infantry F Company

CAPTAIN
Gerhard L. Luhn
FIRST SARGEANT
John D. O'Brien
SARGEANT
William Miller
John H. Neiss
George Russell
CORPORAL
John C. Cain
Ludwig Roper
Lucius E. Stearns
George Wood
MUSICIAN
Peter Cassidy
ARTIFICER
Jay E. Brandow
PRIVATE
Oscar Baker
John Baptiste
Oliver F. Bowden
Edward Buird
Michael Cunningham
Richard Dickson
James Ferguson

William Frisby
John Galliger
George W. Gibbs
William Green
August Gunker
John Healey
William E. Helvie
William Johnston
William Kent
Christopher Larsen
Patrick Lonangan
James Malford
Thomas Malford
David Mesirola
John McCarty
Patrick McEnery
George Richberg
Jacob Schumaker
Oscar Sloan
William Stillwell
Richard C. Sullivan
William Swain
Frederick Tostika
Joseph Turner
William E. Wolfe

Ninth Infantry C Company

CAPTAIN
Samuel Munson
   FIRST LIEUTENANT
Thaddeus H. Capron
   FIRST SARGEANT
James Whelan
   SARGEANT
William W. Butler
Jesse N. Farmer
Stephen Malloy
Andrew J. O'Leary
   CORPORAL
Marshall Crocker
George Kressig
Andrew Murphy
William S. Parsons
   BUGLER
Frank Clarke
   ARTIFICER
William H. Smith
   PRIVATE
Sylvester Blanwell
Howard Boyer
Edward Burns
James W. Butler
William B. Colcroft
Harley Crittenden
Michael Deegan

Christopher Dillion
Edward Donnelly
Michael Dougherty
Charles Edwards
John C. Eisenberg
Barney Flanagan
Samuel Gibson
Thomas W. Granberry
Frank Hamill
Frederick Hanshammer
Solomon Herschberg
Julius Hoppi
Thomas Hughes
Samuel Hunt
Samuel Jacob
Andrew Johnson
David Mahoney
George W. McAnnulty
Hugh McLean
Ernest Melin
Henry Mell
Oliver Navarre
Charles A. Nichols
Calvin Rainsome
Walter C. Smith
Ole Tothamer
Luther B. Wolfe
Albert Zimmerman

Ninth Infantry G Company

CAPTAIN
Thomas B. Burrowes
   FIRST LIEUTENANT
William L. Carpenter
   FIRST SARGEANT
John C. Rafferty
   SARGEANT
Frances Doyle

Frederick Klein
Frank McCarthy
   CORPORAL
James Delaney
Timothy O'Sullivan
Rudolph Ormann
Joseph S. Wrisley
   TRUMPETER

William Doody
Hugh Thomson
ARTIFICER
Joseph Holtz
PRIVATE
John Anderson
Richard L. Case
Edward Conlin
Patrick Dwyer
William Ecrestain
William Faulman
James Gaskill
William E. Glick
William R. Hardin

Michael Healey
August Hocksmith
Frederick Lafine
Gineral A. Lee
Alexander M. Lowrie
Michael Murphy
John G. Newman
John Norton
Samuel Smith
John Thomas
Charles W. Wilson
Samuel H. Woollen
Samuel C. Wynkoop
Rudolph Zysset

Ninth Infantry H Company

CAPTAIN
Andrew S. Burt
SECOND LIEUTENANT
Edgar B. Robertson
FIRST SARGEANT
August Lange
SARGEANT
Charles F. Hiller
Danford R. Langley
John Smith
Henry Stoll
CORPORAL
John McFarlane
Sylvester Poole
TRUMPETER
Bernhard Blomer
Julius Permell
PRIVATE
Louis Allison
John H. Atwood
Joseph S. Bennett

Charles Beyschlag
Samuel B. Brown
George Coy
David N. Eshelman
Henry Robert Fritz
Thaddeus N. Hendricksen
Geroge E. Leggatt
John McCann
John McCormick
James Morgan
William Nobles
Richard O'Hearn
Daniel P. Reddy
Charles Riesch
John Seery
Aaron Smith
John Stephenson
Warren Taylor
John Walsh
Richard Walsh
James Waters
Peter Winegardner

Second Cavalry A Company

CAPTAIN
Thomas B. Dewees
SECOND LIEUTENANT
Daniel C. Pearson
FIRST SARGEANT
Gregory P. Harrington
SEARGENT
Alexander Albrecht
William H. Butterworth
John A. Carr
James Ellis
Charles A. Maude
CORPORAL
Charles Angus
Antonio Brogerri
John Naaf
Charles Wintermute
TRUMPETER
William F. Somers
John W. Vincent
FARRIER
John A. Bott
BLACKSMITH
Bernard Schnable
SADDLER
Frederick France
PRIVATE
Charles Austin
James Branagan
Henry C. Campbell
Marvin Collins
John A. Courtney
Thomas J. Dickinsen
Uriah Donaldson

Michael Duffy
John Durkin
Henry Glock
Hugh Green
George Greenbauer
James Hayes
James P. Henry
John Kelly
Charles King
Ferdinand Knupper
Rudolph Laffelbein
Edward Lewis
Henry A. McCook
James McDuff
Christopher McIntyre
William H. Merritt
Daniel Morgan
Daniel Munger
John Murphy
David W. Neil
Robert Noonan
William F. Norwood
William J. Porter
William L. Regan
Michael Reynolds
George B. Robinson
Thomas A. Second
Charles M. Sheldon
Charles Spencer
George W. Sweeney
John F. Vincent
Alonzo A. Vincent
James Walsh
John Wray

Second Cavalry B Company

FIRST LIEUTENANT
William B. Rawolle
FIRST SARGEANT
Charles S. Alter
SARGEANT
William J. Cunningham
Charles W. Day
John Howard
Thomas Murray
Bartholomew Shannon
CORPORAL
Thomas Aughey
Eugene H. Glasure
Alexander Huntington
James Mitchell
TRUMPETER
Robert Dyer
John Friegel
FARRIER
Charles F. Jones
BLACKSMITH
Edmund Grady
SADDLER
John Graninckstrotkin
PRIVATE
John Atkin
Daniel Austin
Henry Baldwin
Henry Chambers
Henry G. Coffman
William Cogan
Charles P. Corliss
James Corniff
James Cosgriff
Robert Coster

William Coulton
Louis Craft
Richard N. Criswell
William J. Daughty
John Davis
Patrick Doherty
Benjamin Domeck
Charles F. Edwards
Adam Fox
Wesley Gable
Thomas B. Glover
Michael Graemer
Alexander Graham
Paul Gutike
Patrick Hanson
Herman Harold
Francis Hart
William A. Hills
Thomas Kelly
Eggert Kohler
Theodore P. Leighton
William W. Lyman
Daniel McClurg
Henry Morris
Francis O'Connor
Charles S. Podge
James Ramer
Peter J. Redmond
George W. Rowlau
Mark B. Rue
William H. Tailor
Augustus Thompson
George D. Vickers
Patrick Wall
Herbert Witmer

Second Cavalry D Company

FIRST LIEUTENANT
Samuel D. Swigert
SECOND LIEUTENANT
Henry D. Huntington
FIRST SARGEANT
James W. Marcy
SARGEANT
Oscar R. Cornwell
Frederick W. Evans
John L. Joisteen
†Patrick O'Donnell
George C. Williams
CORPORAL
Henry C. Harrington
William Madigar
Russell W. Payne
William I. Webb
TRUMPETER
Gustavus Nicolai
Joseph A. Wadsworth
ARTIFICER
Henri Heynimann
BLACKSMITH
William L. Webb
SADDLER
William H. Haynes
PRIVATES
William Allen
James Anthony
Otis Clark
Davis Connors
Michael Connors
Jeremiah Cory
Samuel J. Curtis
James Darcy
George Daum
Henry DeMott
Edward Devinney

William Dudly
John Flemming
James Forrestel
William Fryling
James Galvin
John T. Harris
Carl Hecht
Samuel W. Hine
Eugene Isaac
John Jackson
Abraham Jacobs
Washington Jones
Harry Kiel
James Koelman
William Lang
Joseph Laverty
John Lewis
John McCormack
George McKnight
William McManus
Jacob Mack
Frank Mackenzie
William Madden
William H. Moffitt
John Moore
Charles E. Parker
John C. Putnam
Emile Renner
John Shields
George A. Stone
Carlton Torman
Joseph Ward
Edward A. Watson
Thomas H. White
William H. Williams
James Wilson
Joseph Wilson
John F.A. Witt

Second Cavalry E Company

CAPTAIN
Elizah R. Wells
SECOND LIEUTENANT
Frederick W. Sibley
FIRST SARGEANT
William Land
SARGEANT
William P. Cooper
Weaver Dollmair
Louis Gilbert
George L. Howard
Orson M. Smith
CORPORAL
John Hollenbacker
William C. Kingsley
Otto C. Mendhoff
TRUMPETER
Peter Waag
SADDLER
Joseph F. Long
PRIVATE
Leo Baader
John Bach
Nicholas Burbach
Patrick Clark
George Coyle
William I. Croley
Lawrence Delaney
William J. Dougherty
George Douglas
Milton F. Douglass
William T. Englehorn

Frank Foster
Daniel Gabriel
John Glancey
Jacob Heird
John Hoffman
David Hogg
Howard Krapp
Austin E. Lemon
Alfred Logan
Gustav Martini
Montgomery McCormick
Thomas McCue
William C. Murray
Edward Nagle
Richard Parkington
William F. Paul
Linden B. Perry
Oliver Remley
Cody Robertson
Oscar Rollan
George Rosendale
Valentine Rufus
Charles H. Sargent
James A. Scott
James Smith
Patrick Sullivan
Charles Tausher
Jeremiah Twiggs
James Vance
William Volmer
Hugo Wagner

Second Cavalry I Company

CAPTAIN
Henry E. Noyes
SECOND LIEUTENANT
Fred W. Kingsbury

FIRST SARGEANT
William Kirkwood
SARGEANT
William Skinner

William Taylor
CORPORAL
Amos Black
Thomas C. Marion
†Thomas Meagher
John P. Slough
FARRIER
George Fisher
SADDLER
Henry Knapper
PRIVATE
Hermann Ashkey
George M. Bickford
Phillipp Burnett
John E. Collins
Charles Emmons
Frank W. Foss
John Gallagher
Charles G. Graham
John G. Hall
Robert Johnson
Walter B. Keenright

Peter King
George H. Liddle
Martin Maher
Charles Minarcik
John Moran
Charles Morrison
Gustav Ohm
James H. Ray
John Reynolds
George Rhode
Gottlieb Ruf
John Russell
Konrad Schmid
John M. Stevenson
Irvine H. Stout
William Strong
Patrick H. Wall
Daniel Walsh
George J. Walters
George Watts
Thomas Wingfield

Third Cavalry A Company

FIRST LIEUTENANT
Joseph Lawson
SECOND LIEUTENANT
Charles Morton
FIRST SARGEANT
John W. Van Moll
SARGEANT
Charles Anderson
William J. Armstrong
Gottlieb Bigalsky
Henry Shafer
Frederick Stanley
CORPORAL
Charles A. Bessey
William H. Finch

John Patton
TRUMPETER
George Hammer
Walter Wells
SADDLER
Karl Dreher
BLACKSMITH
Michael Conway
PRIVATE
James Allen
John Anderson
William Babcock
Conrad Baker
Frederick Bartlett
John Bigley

Robert Blackwood
Joseph Boyle
Maurice Breshnahan
John Cook
William Davis
John Downey
William Featherall
Michael Fitzgerald
James Golden
Charles Gordon
Lawrence L. Grazierni
Edwin M. Griffin
Thomas Gynau
Maurice Hastings
Robert Harry Heinz
Herman J. Kaider
Lawrence Kennedy
Charles Kolaugh

Henry Leonard
John A. Lowder
John Lynch
John McCann
Florence Neiderst
Samuel Peterson
John Reilly
James L. Roberts
Henry Rompton
Albert Simons
James E. Snepp
Alfred S. Southon
James Taggart
Ernest Therion
William H. Vince
John Wenzel
George White
James Wood

Third Cavalry B Company

CAPTAIN
Charles Meinhold
SECOND LIEUTENANT
James F. Simpson
FIRST SARGEANT
Charles Witzemann
SARGEANT
Charles S. Abbott
James A. Boggs
Maurice Connell
John Moriarity
Robert Stewart
CORPORAL
Thomas M. Clarke
George G. Criswell
Joseph Kirby
John Tighe
TRUMPETER
Hugh Carlton

FARRIER
Robert Roulston
SADDLER
Henry N. Tucker
BLACKSMITH
James A. Chaffee
PRIVATE
Conrad Allbright
George Allen
James E. Anderson
William E. Anthon
Charles R. Appleton
William E. Baldwin
John W. Barrow
Joseph Bennett
William Brindley
Edward Bushlepp
James Calvin
James Cleveland

Hugh Curry
John Davis
Michael J. Fitzpatrick
Thomas Flood
Charles Foster
Joseph Gallagher
John W. Hobbs
Francois Jourdain
John Kramer
Andrew Lee
William Lee
William B. Lewis
John Longrigg
Reginald A. Loomis
Franklin A. Maricle
Francis Mayer
Hugh McConnell
Martin M. Moore
Julius Murray

William Pattison
Henry L. Quinn
Robert Rice
John Ritchie
Thomas D. Sanford
Thomas Slater
Frank Smith
John H. Smith
†Henry Steiner
George Stickney
James Sweeney
John H. Thorison
David A. Tilson
William Walton
Francis A. Wilbur
William Wilson
Frederick Winters
Edwin D. Wood

Third Cavalry C Company

CAPTAIN
Frederick Van Vliet
FIRST SARGEANT
William Riley
SARGEANT
Otto Ahrens
Hermann Guenther
Joseph Manly
John J. Mitchell
John Welsh
CORPORAL
Eugene Bessiers
Joseph N. Hobsen
Michael F. Lanigan
William Stewart
TRUMPETER
Alfred Helmbold
George Steele

FARRIER
William Johnson
SADDLER
John Mathews
BLACKSMITH
Heinrich Glucing
WAGGONER
Henry Wellwood
PRIVATE
James Allen
Henry Bartley
George W. Bickford
Henry Burmeister
William B. Dubois
Wentelin Ehrig
Perry A. Elden
Walter Gau
John H. Green

William Hart
William Herd
Henry Johnson
William Larkingland
John D. Leak
Fred Lehman
Arthur Leroy
George P. Lowry
William P. McCandless
William J. McClinton
William McDonald
John Miller
James Mulney
James Nolan
Fred Paul
James Perkins

Frank Quado
John Reed
John W. Reppert
Francis Rodgers
Louis Sachs
George E. Sanderson
John H. Sherman
David O. Sloan
John A. Smith
Harry Snowdon
Andrew Tierney
William M. Walcott
Arnold Weber
Henry Weyworth
George Williams
Louis Zinzer

Third Cavalry D Company

CAPTAIN
†Guy V. Henry
SECOND LIEUTENANT
John G. Bourke
FIRST SARGEANT
Joseph Robinson
SARGEANT
Patrick Flood
John Knox
John D. Lindsay
Richard J. McKee
Charles Taylor
CORPORAL
William Blair
William Ferguson
John McDonald
John F. Sanders
TRUMPETER
Frank Ropetsky
FARRIER
John Robinson

BLACKSMITH
George W. Hutchinson
PRIVATE
Sidney F. Bates
Michael Bolton
James Caraley
Frank Cunningham
Frank DeHaven
John Delmont
John F. Doherty
August Dorn
Charles Dougherty
John W. Elder
Robert Flint
Eugene Jones
John Kearney
James Kelly
Jacob Knittell
James Loun
John McDonald
John Miller

John Phillips
Charles H. Pulli
Thomas Riley
Alfred Rowcliffe
Francis Stahl
George Steine
John Stevens

Dennis Sullivan
Charles Ward
Jacob R. Webb
Frederick Weber
J. Franklin Webster
Henry Wielenburg

Third Cavalry E Company

CAPTAIN
Alexander Sutorius
FIRST LIEUTENANT
A.H. Von Luettwitz
SECOND LIEUTENANT
Henry R. Lemly
FIRST SARGEANT
Jeremiah Foley
SARGEANT
Edward Glass
Morgan B. Hawks
Joseph Nemour
Frank P. Secrist
CORPORAL
Edwin F. Ambrose
William Miller
Charles N.E. Williams
TRUMPETER
George Hoffstetter
Evan S. Worthy
FARRIER
Samuel Stanley
BLACKSMITH
George Hanernas
SADDLER
Peter Jansen
PRIVATE
Daniel Akley
Christopher Ayers
John Beatts

Michael Brannon
Joseph Budka
Henry Burton
William H. Clark
James Conway
Malachi Dillion
Richard Dillion
Andrew Dolfer
Patrick J. Dowling
Orlando H. Duren
Charles F. Eichweitzel
Thomas Ferguson
John Foley
Michael Glannon
Lewis S. Grigsby
Marcus Hansen
Patrick Hennessey
†Henry Herald
William G. Hill
Peter Hollen
Bernard Kelly
Patrick Kelly
John Langan
Edward Lavelle
William C.C. Lewis
Thomas Lloyd
Allen Lupton
Marcus Magerlein
Edward McKiernan
Thomas McNamara

James Montgomery
Thomas Nolan
William Pease
Henry Perkins
Joseph Peterson
James Quinn

William Rice
Daniel C. Ross
William Schubert
Patrick Scully
Alexander Shire
Daniel Timmey

Third Cavalry F Company

SECOND LIEUTENANT
Bainbridge Reynolds
FIRST SARGEANT
Michael A. McGann
SARGEANT
Robert Emmet
John Gross
Thomas Hackett
*David Marshall
Frank Rugg
John C.A. Warfield
CORPORAL
John Fry
Dennis Giles
John Kohn
TRUMPETER
Arthur N. Chamberlin
FARRIER
Richard O'Grady
BLACKSMITH
Averius S. Varney
SADDLER
Jeremiah Murphy
PRIVATE
Spencer Bates
†Otto Brodersen
Henry Carson
William Chambers
Thomas Cramer
Charles Dennis
Michael T. Donahue

Peter Dyke
Frank W. Estabrook
†William Featherly
Edward Glasheen
John Hecker
Frederick Hershler
Julius Jansen
John W. Jordan
Henry Kett
John Lannen
David Lindsay
Robert Livingston
Richard Lynch
Michael McGraine
Oliver Meserby
John Meyer
James Moran
William Mulroy
John Murphy
Alexander Noterman
Gerold O'Grady
Michael O'Hearne
*Gilbert Roe
Ferdinand Rutten
Albert Salice
John Semple
John Staley
John Tischer
†Phineas Towne
Charles R. West
Francis Woltering

Third Cavalry G Company

FIRST LIEUTENANT
Emmet Crawford
FIRST SARGEANT
William Campbell
SARGEANT
William Conklin
Hugo Deprizin
Fritz W. Henry
William Mason
CORPORAL
Jacob Bender
Fred Gahlsdorf
Allen J. Rosenberry
TRUMPETER
Joseph Billow
Robert McMurray
FARRIER
Patrick Tooel
BLACKSMITH
Charles P. Hansen
SADDLER
Charles F. Smith
WAGONER
Frank McConnell
PRIVATE
James H. Bell
Hubert Beohnke
John B. Comber
Edward M. Courtney
Patrick Delmage
George M. Edgar
Frederick P. English
Henry Feister

Byron D. Ferguson
Frederick W.S. Fonss
Patrick Freeman
James Gandley
Thomas Glanon
John Hale
Edwin Hamilton
Jacob Hekel
Alonzo Hogland
Adolph Kalber
Thomas Kirby
Edward C. Leitelt
John Martin
James McChesney
John McClain
Edward McCloskey
John Miner
William Moore
Henry Olsson
Gotthilf Osterday
Thomas Phelan
Thomas Quinn
Fred Ray
James E. Rose
Charles W. Ruffle
Henry Schmidt
Peter Schweikart
John Smith
William Smith
George Spreight
John A. Taylor
William Taylor
James Welsh

Third Cavalry I Company

CAPTAIN
William H. Andrews

FIRST LIEUTENANT
Albert King

SECOND LIEUTENANT
James E.H. Foster
FIRST SARGEANT
John Henry
SARGEANT
Peter Foster
†Andrew Grosh
George W. Lowry
Johh Sullivan
CORPORAL
Frederick Ashwall
John I. Byrons
Tobias Carty
William H. West
FARRIER
Michael O'Reilley
BLACKSMITH
Dick C. Kingston
SADDLER
Frank S. Connells
PRIVATE
*William Allen
Henry Blake
George H. Bowers
Peter Butler
John Carroll
John Conley
Edward Flood, Jr.
*Eugene Flynn

Benjamin Heald
Charles H. Hines
Frank W. Hitchcock
George Holledered
John Hubert
James M. Hurt
Anselm Langman
William Leary
†John Losciborski
Frank Maginn
James Martin
Michael McMahon
Robert Neal
†James O'Brien
Robert F. Pratt
William Ray
†James Reilley
Robert Roberts
Patrick Ryan
William Schubert
Daniel Shields
Lewis C. Singleton
†Francis Smith
John Smith II
Fritz Strickert
†Charles W. Stuart
Herbert W. Weaver
Thomas Welch
Louis Wilmer

Third Cavalry L Company

CAPTAIN
Peter D. Vroom
SECOND LIEUTENANT
George F. Chase
FIRST SARGEANT
Joseph Howe
SARGEANT
Fuller H. Chepperson

†Samuel Cook
*Anton Newkirken
Roswell E. Patterson
CORPORAL
David H. Connell
Eugene Prince
Otto Tigerstraim
Edward Walker

TRUMPETER
†William H. Edwards
Marcellus Goddard
BLACKSMITH
Charles Webster
FARRIER
George B. Oaks
SADDLER
Charles L. Fisk
PRIVATE
*Richard Bennett
Henry J. Bowler
Richard Callahan
Christopher Camp
Michael Cassidy
John Clements
*Brooks Connors
John Creme
William Griffith
John Hanrahan
Daniel Harrigan
Thomas Hill
Harrison Hiricer
†John Kremer
Theodore Lowe

Fred Mayer
Thomas F. Maxwell
George H. McDonald
Charles Miller
William Miller
*Allen J. Mitchell
James O'Donnell
James L. Parks
Louis Phister
*George Potts
George Ray
Antony Schenkberg
Claud Schmidt
George A. Serila
John T. Smith
George Sproul
Michel Sullivan
James F. Todd
Thomas Walker
William M. Ward
Richard H. White
Rudolph Winn
Azabel R. Van Seer
Alexander Yates

Third Cavalry M Company

CAPTAIN
Anson Mills
FIRST LIEUTENANT
Augustus C. Paul
SECOND LIEUTENANT
Fred Schwatka
FIRST SARGEANT
Frank Rittel
SARGEANT
Alexander B. Ballard
Frank V. Erhard
Charles Kaminski

Franklin B. Robinson
CORPORAL
Gilbert Exford
Mathew Grappenstetter
Peter L. Hogebroom
John A. Kirkwood
TRUMPETER
Frank Serfas
†Elmer A. Snow
BLACKSMITH
Albert Glaurniski
SADDLER

Charles H. Lindenberg
  PRIVATE
Henry Badgery
Myron P. Boyer
John H. Bryce
Carlos L. Chamberlin
Bernard F. Cullen
Henry E. Curley
Bernard Deringer
John E. Douglass
Dave S. Drake
Dennis B. Duggan
Geroge Foster
John A. Foster
Isaac J. Kelton
Dennis W. Larkin
Patrick I. Maguire
Hugh H. Massey
Timothy McCarthy
William McGinness

James B. Miller
Joseph W. Morgan
Albert Morganthaler
Jeremiah Murphy
Thomas I. O'Keefe
Adam Pringle
George Raab
Dave C. Renear
William H. Reynolds
Blaseus Schmalz
Joseph Schmittz
Fred Schuttle
James Shanley
John W. Singer
Robert Smith
John I. Stevenson
John Sweeney
Charles E. Trevick
Soren O. Very
Joseph Walzer

CASUALTIES AT ROSEBUD JUNE 17, 1876

Return of killed, wounded and missing of the troops serving under command of Brig Genl Geo Crook in the action with hostile Sioux on Rosebud River June 17, 1876. (Report of General Crook in Vaughn Collection Coe Library, U. of Wyoming, Laramie.)

NAME	RANK	CO.	REGIMENT	KILLED OR WOUNDED	REMARKS
1. Marshall, David	Sgt.	F	3rd Cav.	Killed	Buried on Rosebud River
2. Roe, Gilbert	Pvt.	F	3rd Cav.	Killed	Buried on Rosebud River
3. Allen, William	Pvt.	I	3rd Cav.	Killed	Buried on Rosebud River
4. Flynn, Eugene	Pvt.	I	3rd Cav.	Killed	Buried on Rosebud River
5. Newkirken, Anton	Sgt.	L	3rd Cav.	Killed	Buried on Rosebud River
6. Bennett, Richard	Pvt.	L	3rd Cav.	Killed	Buried on Rosebud River
7. Potts, George	Pvt.	L	3rd Cav.	Killed	Buried on Rosebud River
8. Connors, Brooks	Pvt.	L	3rd Cav.	Killed	Buried on Rosebud River
9. Mitchell, Allen J.	Pvt.	L	3rd Cav.	Killed	Buried on Rosebud River
1. Henry, Guy V.	Capt.	D	3rd Cav.	Wounded	Minie bullet, severe gunshot wound in both maxillars fractured.
2. O'Donnell, Patrick	Sgt.	D	2nd Cav.	Wounded	Several gunshot wounds
3. Meagher, Thomas	Cpl.	I	2nd Cav.	Wounded	Slight wound, gunshot right forearm
4. Steiner, Henry	Pvt.	B	3rd Cav.	Wounded	Severe gunshot left shoulder. Fracture of scapula
5. Herald, Horace[1]	Pvt.	E	3rd Cav.	Wounded	Severe gunshot right shoulder and jaw fracture lower maxillar

6. Brodersen, Otto	Pvt.	F	3rd Cav.	Wounded	Slight wound — not treated
7. Featherly, Wm.	Pvt.	F	3rd Cav.	Wounded	Severe gunshot left arm
8. Towne, Phineas	Pvt.	F	3rd Cav.	Wounded	Pistol bullet severe gunshot abdomen — bullet remained in abdomen
9. Grosch, Andrew	Sgt.	I	3rd Cav.	Wounded	Minie bullet — very severe gunshot left arm and chest both arms fractured
10. Carty, Tobias[2]	Cpl.	I	3rd Cav.	Wounded	Slight, not carried on sick report
11. Smith, Francis	Pvt.	I	3rd Cav.	Wounded	Severe gunshot right leg. Fracture of tibula
12. Stuart, Charles	Pvt.	I	3rd Cav.	Wounded	Severe gunshot wound left wrist and arm
13. O'Brien, James	Pvt.	I	3rd Cav.	Wounded	Severe gunshot wound left forearm
14. Losciborski, John	Pvt.	I	3rd Cav.	Wounded	Severe gunshot wound right elbow-fracture
15. Cook, Samuel	Sgt.	L	3rd Cav.	Wounded	Severe gunshot wound left thigh
16. Edwards, William	Trump	L	3rd Cav.	Wounded	Severe gunshot wound left thigh
17. Kremer, John	Pvt.	L	3rd Cav.	Wounded	Severe gunshot wound shoulder fractured
18. Snow, Elmer	Trump	M	3rd Cav.	Wounded	Severe gunshot wound, wrist of right arm fractured wrist bones and arm
19. Devine, James	Pvt.	D	4th Inf.	Wounded	Slight gunshot wound of head. bone fracture
20. Terry, John	Pvt.	D	4th Inf.	Wounded	Slight gunshot wound left leg. Tibia and Fibular fracture
21. Flynn, Richard	Pvt.	D	4th Inf.	Wounded	Slight gunshot wound left shoulder.

---

[1] Listed as Henry Herald on Muster Roll

[2] Company Returns do not show Carty among wounded. Pvt. James Reilley of same Company is listed as wounded but does not appear on this one.

Appendix C

Following the Rosebud fight, Crook and many of his officers submitted reports of the battle. These reports are now on file in the National Archives. Copies of the reports have appeared in *With Crook at the Rosebud*, *The Battle of the Rosebud Plus Three*, and *Before the Little Big Horn*. Reports either were not filed or have been lost for company commanders Captain Peter Vroom, Alexander Sutorious, Lieutenant Bainbridge Reynolds and Emmett Crawford.

OFFICIAL REPORT OF GENERAL CROOK

Headquarters Big Horn and Yellowstone Expedition
Camp Cloud Peak
Base Big Horn Mountains W.T.
June 20, 1876

To the
  Assistant Adjutant General
    Headquarters Mil Dis of the Mo.
      Chicago, Ills.

Sir
  I have the honor to report that the detachments of Crow and Shoshone Indian Scouts I had been negotiating for, reached me the

night of the 14th instant. I immediately packed my trains, pack animals etc in a secure place so arranged that the civilian employes left with them, could if necessary, defend them till our return, and marched on the morning of the 16th with every available fighting man and four days rations carried by each officer and man on his person or saddle. I allowed no lead horses, each officer and man being equipped alike, with one blanket only, and every man who went whether citizen, servant or soldier, armed and with some organization for fighting purposes only.

The Crow Indians were under the impression that the hostile village was located on Tongue River or some of its small tributaries and were quite positive we should be able to surprise it. While I hardly believe this to be possible as the Indians had hunting parties out who must necessarily become aware of the presence of the command, I considered it worth while to make the attempt. The Indians (ours) of course being expert in this matter I regulated movements entirely by their efforts to secure this end.

Marching from our camp on the South Fork of Tongue River, or Goose Creek as sometimes called, towards the Yellowstone on the end of the first days march we came to a small stream near the divide that separates the waters of the Tongue and Rosebud we discovered that a small party of hunters had seen us. We crossed the divide that evening and camped on the headwaters of a small stream laid down on the map as Rosebud Creek and about thirty five or forty miles from our camp on Tongue River.

Pushing on the next morning down the Rosebud with my Indian scouts in front, when about five miles down the stream, near the mouth of the canon, the scouts came into camp reported that they had seen something, and wished me to go into camp where we were lying close till they could investigate, and very soon after others came in reporting the Sioux in the vicinity and within a few minutes we were attacked by them in force.

The country was very rough and broken the attack made in greater or less force on all sides, and in advancing to meet it the command necessarily became separated. Under the circumstances I did not believe that any fight we could have would be decisive in its result, unless we secured their village supposed to be in close proximity. I therefore made every effort to close the command and march on their village.

I had great difficulty in getting the battalions together, each command being pressed by the Indians as the effort to concentrate them was made, the roughness of the ground facilitating this. The Indians apparently being aware of the reason of the movement and assembling on the bluffs overlooking the canon through which the command would have to pass.

While the engagement was in progress I succeeded however in throwing a portion of the command into and down the canon for several miles but was obliged to use it elsewhere and before the entire command was concentrated it was believed that the canon was well covered. Our Indians refusing to go into it saying it would be certain death. The bluffs on the side of the canon being covered with timber they could fire upon the command at short range while a return fire would be of no effect.

The troops having repulsed the attack and in connection with the Indian Scout drove the Sioux several miles and our Indians refusing to go down the canon to the supposed location of the village, it remained to follow the retreating Sioux without rations, dragging our wounded after us on rough mule litters, or return to our train where they could be cared for, the latter being the course adopted we camped that night on the field, and marched next morning, and reaching camp yesterday evening, having been absent as intended when we first started four days.

Our casualties during the action, were 10 killed including one Indian Scouts, and 21 wounded, including Captain Guy V. Henry, 3rd Cavalry, severely wounded in the face. It is impossible to correctly estimate the loss of the enemy as the field extended over several miles of rough country including rocks and ravines, not examined by us after the fight. Thirteen of their dead bodies being left in close proximity to our lines.

I respectfully call attention to the enclosed reports of Lieut. Colonel Royall, 3rd Cavalry and Major Chambers, 4th Infantry, commanding the Cavalry and Infantry battalions respectively and commend the gallantry and efficiency of the officers and men of the expedition as worthy of every praise.

Lieut. Col Royall and Major Chambers have given me great strength by the able manner in which they commanded their respective columns.

I am particularly grateful to them for their efficiency during the trip and the engagement.

> I am Sir
> Very Respectfully
> Your Obedt Servt
> (Signed)   George Crook
> Brigadier General Commanding

OFFICIAL REPORT OF MAJOR ANDREW W. EVANS

Camp on South Goose Creek
June 20, 1876

Act. Asst. Adjt. Genl
Hd Qrs Cavalry, G, H, and Y Exp:

Sir,

In compliance with your instructions to report the part taken by the battalion, 3rd Cavalry, in the engagement with Indians on the 17th inst. I have the honour to do so, as follows: so far as the same came under my observation: The command marching down Rosebud Cr. on the morning of the day, had halted & unsaddled about three miles below the camping ground of the night before, when an alarm of the approach of hostile Indians was given, who soon made their appearance over a high hill to the N.W. Immediately after saddling I sent Capt Van Vliet's squadron (C & G Cos) to occupy the commanding ridge on the S, and Capt Henry was directed to place two Cos a short distance up the creek, on a lower ridge commanding the approach down the valley in that direction. He obeyed by going with his own Co. for one of these. The positions thus taken up were all on the right bank of the creek, on which side the 3rd had been marching. The battalion was then directed to cross the creek to the left bank (crossing bad and boggy); and receiving no further orders it was massed behind a low hill: in numbers six Cos; being Capt Mills' battalions and two cos of Henrys. I rode up to another ridge on the left front, to observe the engagements then going on, and had scarcely reached its crest when I was followed by Col. Royall, leading the six cos in column, who directed me to deploy them as skirmishers in line forward and then proceeded to the front with his staff. I was endeavoring to deploy Mills' cos, when the command was again thrown forward in column, I believe by Col Royall's direct order, going up the hills at a rapid gallop & leaving me necessarily in the rear. followed as speedily as my horse would carry me to the high ridge where the enemy had first appeared & where I supposed Col Royall had gone. He had however inclined to the left, followed by Cos. B & L of Henry's battalions & I of Mills', and I found on the ridge only the latter with three Cos (A, E & M) deployed as skirmishers dismounted, and exchanging distant shots with the enemy. I was directed by Genl Crook to withdraw this line, a little while after, to mount & to prepare for a movement upon the Indian village (supposed to be in the neighbourhood), but I was obliged upon pressure from the enemy to reestablish it. By Genl Crook's order I also withdrew Van Vliet & was joined by him upon the hill in due time. Subsequently, the engagement slackening on this side, Capt Mills, with his three cos, was detached by Genl Crook under special orders, and moved down the hills, and I was ordered to hold another portion of the ridge with Capt Van Vliet's squadron, where, however, no firing worth mentioning was encountered. Meanwhile Col Royall, hotly engaged on the far left & front, had ordered to join him Henry's two Cos (F & D), withdrawing them from the position where I had placed them; and of the operations of the five cos (B, D, F, I & L) I had only a distant & imperfect view. The Cavalry Commander, Col Royall, under whose personal orders they were, knows best how well they behaved. I regret exceedingly that Capt Henry's severe wound renders it quite out of the question that he should make a written report of the operations of his battalion. The reports of Capts Mills & Van Vliet are enclosed herewith. The subsequent movement of the day, after the withdrawal of the Indians, are not, I presume, included in your instructions. The casualties in the 3rd Cav were one officer, (Col Henry) severely wounded; 9 enlisted men killed & 17 wounded. Upon reviewing the above my attention is called that the withdrawal, by Col. Royall, of the two Cos of Henry from the position in which I had placed them in the valley, took place before the charge up the hill. I need scarcely add that throughout the affair the officers & men of the Reg't conducted themselves with great coolness & gallantry. Of the 5 Cos with Col Royall, it is proper to mention that one (B- Capt Meinhold) was sent off by him under orders, and joined me on the high ridge before the close of the fight. Capt Meinhold has taken down from Col Henry's lips his report of the operations of his battalion previous to his wound, and supplemented this by a report of its subsequent movement: both of which are enclosed.

> Very Respectfully
> Your Obt Serv't
> A.W. Evans, Major 3rd Cavalry

OFFICIAL REPORT OF CAPTAIN HENRY E. NOYES

Camp on Goose Creek, Wyo. Ty
June 20th, 1876

Lieut. H.R. Lemly. 3rd Cavalry
 Adjutant Cavalry Battalions

Sir

In obedience To Par II of Circular of this date from HdQrs Battalion 2nd and 3rd Cavalry, I have the honor to respectfully report that my command was resting at the first halting place after leaving Camp on the 17th inst. the horses being unsaddled and grazing, in obedience to orders received. We had been unsaddled but a short time when I received orders to saddle up and await further orders. The Battalion was but just saddled, when some of the friendly Indians came running over the bluffs, at the foot of which we were, and by their words and actions informed us that the Sioux were coming in large numbers. As there was considerable discharging of firearms in the direction indicated, and every sign of the close proximity of the Sioux, Without awaiting further orders, I ordered four of the five companies of my Battalion forward on foot, leaving Co. A (Capt Dewees) in charge of the led horses of the other campanies. We reached the top of the bluff as soon as possible, and drove the Sioux from the part of the ridge to the left of the ravine that cut through it (and at the mouth of which we had been resting). Company D (Lieut. Swigert) was posted on the knob to the right of this ravine which was very rough and rocky and afforded cover for quite a number of Sioux.

Company E (Capt Wells) was posed on the knob and crest to the left of this ravine, and the other two companies (Co B. Lieut Rawolle, and I, Lieut. Kingsbury) were on the ridge to the left of Co. E. Co. D reached the crest just before the arrival of the Sioux, who were found in force just beyond. The companies to the left of this ravine found the Sioux on the crest, but drove them from it and they retreated toward our left along the crest , whence they were subsequently driven by troops further to the left.

The command was halted on the crest to await orders: the only casualties attending the occupation of this ridge was the wounding of First Sergeant Thomas Meagher, Co. I. 2nd Cavalry, and Sergeant Patrick O'Donnell, Co. D. 2nd Cavalry, each of whom was wounded in the arm.

In about an hour, Capt Dewees reported with the led horses, having been ordered forward by the Brigadier General commanding. Not long after the arrival of the led horses, I received an order (through Lieut Bourke A.D.C.) to withdraw my command from the crest, mount and follow Capt Mills' battalion down the creek. This was done without delay, and the Battalion had been travelling very rapidly for about half an hour, in the direction ordered, when Capt Nickerson A.D.C. overtook us and recalled us to rejoin the command. Which we did, cutting across the country and passing over the ground on which the Sioux had been but a short time previous. On the way back I saw a large party of Sioux, leaving the field, a mile or more to our right and rear. After rejoining the command, we marched a short distance toward the front, halted a short time, and countermarched to a camp where we had been resting when the affair commenced. I saw nothing in the conduct of either officers, or men, of my command, but that was deserving of commendation.

The amount of ammunition expended averaged about twelve rounds per man. There were present nine officers and two hundred and sixty enlisted men of the Second Cavalry.

I am, Sir

Very Respectfully
Your Obedient Servant
Henry E. Noyes
Captain 2nd Cavalry
Comdg Battalion 2nd Cavy

OFFICIAL REPORT OF MAJOR ALEX CHAMBERS

Hdgqrs Infantry Battalions B.H. & Y Expedition
Camp Goose Creek June 20, 1876

Acting Asst. Adjutant General
  Big Horn and Yellowstone Expeditions

Sir:

I have the honor to make the following report of the part taken by the Infantry battalion composed of Companies D and F 4th Infantry, and C G and H 9th Infantry in the four (4) days scout of the troops composing the B.H. and Y. Expedition.

The command left camp on Goose Creek, mounted on mules, at 6 o'clock A.M., and marched about thirty five (35) miles to headwaters of Rosebud. Marched the morning of the 17th about five (5) miles and camped. A short time after camping, shots were heard behind the bluffs in rear of camp, and cries that hostile Indians were coming. I sent, as ordered, two companies, dismounted to the edge of the bluffs to protect that point: posted as skirmishers. Shortly after the three (3) remaining companies formed a skirmish line on top of the ridge. After occupying this position for some time. I was ordered to have the Battalion mounted, and marched to the crest of the ridge, which was done, as soon as the companies on the skirmish line could be recalled for that purpose, one retiring for their animals, and the mules of the other companies, the men and animals being kept concealed as much as possible. The left of the cavalry line returning closely pursued by the Indians. Two (2) companies of the 9th Infantry, G and H were sent to protect the withdrawal of Cavalry. The three companies remaining were sent as a skirmish line across the plateau to drive off a body of Indians, behind a conical hill, who kept up constant fire. This was successfully accomplished, and the Indians disappeared. I then took up a position on the hill and remained until 7 P.M., when the command returned to camp on the banks of the river. The command marched next day in rear, to head of creek or branch of Tongue River twenty (20) miles. Next day twenty (20) miles, to near the camp left on the 16th.

Each of the command performed this duty cheerfully and with credit. Casualties were, three enlisted men wounded of Company D 4th Infantry viz: Corporal James A. Devine wounded in head. Private John H. Terry severely wounded in left leg. Private Richard Flynn slightly wounded in left shoulder. For detailed reports I respectfully refer to reports of company commanders, enclosed.

> I am sir very respectfully
> Your Obedient Servant.
> (Sgd) Alex Chambers
> Major 4th Infantry
> Commanding

OFFICIAL REPORT OF CAPTAIN SAMUEL MUNSON

Co C 9th Infantry

Goose Creek (Upper Part)
B.H. and Y. Expedition
June 20th, 1876

The Adjutant
  Infantry Battn.

Sir.

I have the honor to submit the following report for the information of the commanding officer, Infantry Battn, Big Horn and Yellowstone Expedition.

On the morning of the 17th June 1876, Co C 9th Infantry, was unsaddled when the firing on the bluffs commenced. I immediately formed my company as previously directed and waited for orders. The first order I received was to take my men dismounted up the bluffs and report to General Crook. I took my Co to point indicated, but, did not find the General. The men were directed to lie down on the edge of the bluffs and reserve their fire until the Indians had approached near them. At this time I formed part of the line of Infy. and Cavalry holding the second line of bluffs. Before we had time to accomplish anything I was ordered to go back into the valley, saddle up, and then take the Co to the shelter of the nearest hill, and wait for orders. This I did and when joined by two other companies we were directed to proceed up the hill, which we did advancing about 1 ½ miles; at this point we remained for some time. During this halt, the call was given for help, and I was directed to take six of my men, sharpshooters, to some rocks and broken ground on the crest of the hill, and drive back the Sioux who were then charging. This I did, and held the position with the aid of about a dozen men of other companies and about twenty friendly Indians. We were then preparing to form a skirmish line. When this line was formed, my company occupied the right, my skirmishers taking up the ground between the top of the hill and valley below. We met no resistance on that side of the hill — the Sioux retiring — a few only showing themselves at long distance. The action being over, we were ordered to the top of the hill which we occupied until dark. No officers or man of Co C, 9 Infantry was injured.

I have the honor to be Sir Your obedient Servant
S. Munson Captain Commanding Co C 9th Infantry

OFFICIAL REPORT OF CAPTAIN T.B. BURROWES

Co. G 9th Infantry

Camp on Goose Creek W.T.
June 20th, 1876.

Adjutant Batt Inf
In the field

Sir

In compliance with verbal instructions, this day received from your Head Qrs. I have the honor to submit the following report. Company G 9th Inf. consisting of Captain T.B. Burrowes 9th Inf. commanding, 1st Lieut. W.L. Carpenter 9th Inf. with thirty one enlisted men formed part of the Big Horn and Yellowstone Expedition against the Sioux. The Company left the camp of the expedition, on Goose Creek, as a portion of the Infantry Battalion, as mounted Infantry, on the morning of the 16th Inst. at 1 o'clock A.M. Company marched to the head of the Rose Bud Creek that day camped at 9 P.M. distance marched 37 miles. On the morning of the 17th Inst. Company marched 4 miles down the Rose Bud Creek, and at 8:30 A.M. was ordered into action against the Sioux. Company remained in action and under desultory fire for about 4 hours. At about 10:30 A.M. Company was

ordered forward to check advance of Indians on retiring line. —
Advance was made and Indians checked. After the engagement
Company remained on picket duty until nightfall, when it was ordered
to camp with the remainder of the column. Company marched with
expedition on the 18th inst. forming a part of the rear guard of the
column; camped on a tributary of the Tongue River, distance marched
20 miles. On the 19th inst. Company returned with expedition to
supply camp on Goose Creek W. T. distance marched 22 miles.

Casualties in company during engagement on the 17th inst. none.

I am Sir very respectfully

                         Your Obt. Servant
                         T.B. Burrowes
                         Captain 9th Infantry Company G

OFFICIAL REPORT OF CAPTAIN A.S. BURT

                    Co. H 9th Infantry

                                        Camp Goose Creek
                                         June 20, 1876

Lieut. Seaton
   Batt. Adjutant

Sir:

In obedience to orders I forward following report of the four days
scout of my company to the Rosebud and return. On the 15th I was
ordered to receive from Capt Fleury Q.M. necessary number of mules
and saddles to mount my company which after much vexations delay
was accomplished. On the 16th my company as a part of Col Chambers
Batt marched thirty six miles to Rosebud Creek. On the 17th about 8
o'clock A.M. while in camp our Crow Scouts discovered the Sioux

Indians in force near by. My company with rest of Inft. Batt. fell in dismounted and occupied adjacent hills, expecting the Crow and Snake Indians to draw the Sioux by feigned retreat to this position. We were discovered and this plan frustrated. Shortly after this, orders were received to return to camp and mount my company and join Col. Chambers on the hill; which was done in about an hour. This length of time was taken up because of report made to me by Lieut. Seaton of wounded men being in camp and that my company was the last there. I directed him to report to me when the surgeon was ready to move with every wounded man. This was done and then my company, the wounded and the mules of D. Co. 4th Infty moved out and to the hill.

Subsequently while waiting on this hill in line I received orders with Maj. Burrowes "to stop those Indians and occupy that ridge." The ridge referred to was across a ravine and toward the left of the general line some several hundred yard away. The Indians were the Sioux pursuing a battalion of cavalry. We dismounted and moved forward at double time and on reaching the ridge stopped the Indians quickly and decisively without loss on our part, my company disabled two Indians and three ponies. I make this statement carefully believing greater damage was done the enemy. On the evening of the 17th my company went into the old camp on Rosebud Creek. On the 18th my company as part of Col. Chambers Battalion marched 22 miles across Wolf Mountains and camped on a small stream emptying into Tongue River.

On the 19th we returned to camp on Goose Creek. Distance marched 25 miles. Total enlisted men of the company who took part in the scout was 32; 5 sergeants, 2 corporals, 2 buglers and 23 privates. Lieut. Robertson, the non commissioned officers; Buglers and Privates of my company did their duty on the Rosebud Scout.

I am respt-

> Yrobt Svt-
> A.S. Burt
> Captain commanding Co. H, 9th
> Inf.

OFFICIAL REPORT OF CAPTAIN A.B. CAIN

Co. D, 4th Infantry

Big Horn Expedition
Camp on Goose Creek W.T.
  June 20, 1876
Lieut. Henry Seton, 4th Infantry
Adjutant Infantry Battalion

Sir:

I have the honor to submit the following report:

My Company D, 4th Infantry moved from camp on Rosebud Creek, W.T. at about 8 A.M. on the 17th instant, and as skirmishers engaged the enemy Sioux Indians and assisted the Crow and Snake Indians in driving them from their position. My loss was two Privates wounded.

At about 11 A.M. my Company D with Company F 4th Infantry, Captain Luhn and Lieut. Seton, Company C 9th Infantry, Captain Munson and Lieut. Capron, all under my immediate command, moved upon the enemy, and drove him from his position. My loss was one (1) private wounded.

This command was then relieved from the line by a cavalry force.

The officers and enlisted men are entitled to great credit for their good conduct. I respectfully call attention to the following named officers and enlisted men for their gallantry and bravery. Captain Munson and Lieut. Capron 9th Infantry. Captain Luhn and Lieut. Seton 4th Infantry. 1st Sergeant Dexter, Sergeant Lister, Corporals Funk and Conboy, and Private Terry Co D 4th Infantry.

I am Sir Very Respectfully Your Obediant Servant

A.B. CAIN
Captain 4th Infantry Comds
Company D.
Camp Goose Creek
June 20, 1876

OFFICIAL REPORT OF G.L. LUHN

Co. F, 4th Infantry

To the Adjutant Infantry Battalion
  B H & Y Expedition

Sir:

I have the honor to report that Company F 4th Infantry consisting of one (1) commissioned, six (6) non commissioned, officers, and thirty three (33) privates, mounted on mules with four (4) days rations and one hundred rounds of ammunition per man, took the following part in a four (4) days campaign against the Sioux from Goose Creek.

Left camp on Goose Creek on the morning of the 16th inst. marched to Rosebud and camped: left camp about 6 A.M. on the 17th marched about five (5) miles, when the Battle of the Rosebud commenced. The company was deployed as skirmishers and remained on the field until sundown, then marched to the Creek and camped: left camp on the 18th about 6:30 A.M. and marched to Rosebud Mountain and camped: left camp abut 6 A.M. on the 19th and marched to Goose Creek.

Very Respectfully
Your Obdt Servant
G.L. Luhn
Captain F Company 4th Infantry
comdg Company

OFFICIAL REPORT OF LT. COLONEL, W.B. ROYALL

3rd Cavalry

Headquarters Cavalry Battalions, Big Horn & Yellowstone Expedition
Camp South Fork Tongue River W.T.
June 20, 1876

Acting Assitant Adjutant General
Big Horn and Yellowston Expedition

Sir:

In compliance with revised Army Regulations and the verbal instructions of the Brigadier General Commanding I have the honor to submit the following report of the part taken by my command in the engagement with Sioux Indians on the 17th instant.

The Battalions of the Third Cavalry were upon the south bank of the Rosebud River, that of the second being upon the opposite side, when the alarm was given by allied Indians Scouts. Shortly after, firing was heard upon the high crest north of the river and receiving orders to cross, deploy as skirmishers , charge and occupy the hills in the possession of the enemy, those instructions were promptly obeyed. The battalion of the Second Cavalry had already deployed and charged and with Captain Mills' battalions (except Captain Andrews' (I) Company) and Captain Van Vliets squadron of the Third Cavalry, were not under my immediate command at any time during the engagement. Captain Mills' battalion deployed and Captain Van Vliets squadron occupied a crest in rear, but the latter was subsequently removed by the Brigadier General Commanding.

I now found myself upon the extreme left with Captain Andrews' company and Captain Henry's battalion of the Third Cavalry (consisting of companies D, B, L and F commanded respectively by Captains Henry and Meinhold and Lieutenants Vroom and Reynolds of that regiment) the Indians occupying the series of ridges in our immediate front. They were steadily charged and retreated from one crest to another, my instructions at this time being to slowly advance. But few shots were fired the men being mounted. In this manner was reached the ridge lying adjacent to but separated by a wide canon from the main crest, which, the men being dismounted and deployed and the horses protected upon the contiguous slope, I occupied by instructions from an Aide-de-Camp of the Brigadier General Commanding, who informed me that a charge would be made upon the enemy's left flank by the Battalion of the Second Cavalry. The enemy occupied the crest in my immediate front and were promptly engaged. They also lined a battle upon the left distant about six hundred yards from which they obtained a plunging and enfilading fire. Capt Andrews whose company had advanced upon the extreme left, was withdrawn for better protection and a flank and rear movement by the enemy being observed, it was promptly checked by Captain Henry's company which took possession of a rocky ledge to my left and rear.

Immediately subsequent to the delivery of the preceding instructions, I was directed by the Brigadier General Commanding, through an orderly, to extend my right and connect with the left of the main body occupying a remote portion of the highest crest and I detached Captain Meinhold's company for that purpose. I now received an order to withdraw delivered by an Aide-de-camp of the Brigadier General Commanding which I proceeded to obey by gradually retiring my led horses under the protection of a line of skirmishers which movement being perceived by the enemy, they began to close in upon us in large numbers and the ground being favorable for that purpose we were now subjected to a severe direct flank and rear fire. The advance points of the main crest which had before been occupied by troops, had by their withdrawal fallen into the possession of the enemy, observing which, knowing that my successful withdrawal was greatly endangered thereby and my experience in Indian warfare warning me that protection would be necessary in crossing the last defile which separated me from the main command, I dispatched my Adjutant to the Brigadier General Commanding requesting such assistance, but before it was furnished, the enemy (being elsewhere disengaged) was upon us in full force and I was compelled to direct the company commanders to rejoin the main body as rapidly as possible. Thus far my casualties had been slight, but in effecting the crossing the firing was exceedingly severe and my loss quadrupled. For protection in the passage I had directed Lieutenant Vroom and company to precede and line a crest which covered it; but by this time every Sioux in the engagement was surrounding this single battalion and the position assigned was too exposed to be even temporarily occupied. The only killed were in this battalion under my immediate command and numbered nine. There were thirteen wounded including Captain Guy V. Henry 3rd Cavalry, a total of twenty two casualties. In the companies of the 3rd Cavalry not with me during the engagement, there were two men wounded and also two in the Battalion 2nd Cavalry making a total of twenty six casualties in the cavalry. The officers under my command were 2nd Lieutenant Henry R. Lemly Adjutant 2nd Lieutenant Charles Morton A.A. Captains Guy V. Henry and William H. Andrews. 1st Lieutenant Peter D. Vroom and 2nd Lieutenants Bainbridge Reynolds and James E.H. Foster all of the Third Cavalry, their conduct and that of the enlisted men was commendable in every respect. Mr. R.B. Davenport of the New York *Herald* accompanied me throughout the entire engagement. The report of Major Andrew W. Evans 3rd Cavalry and Captain H.E. Noyes 2nd Cavalry are appended.

Very Respectfully Your Obdt. Servt.

(Sigd) W.B. Royall

Lieutenant Colonel 3rd Cavalry

Commaning

OFFICIAL REPORT OF CHARLES MEINHOLD

Co. B, 3rd Cavalry
Camp on South Fork of Tongue River W. T.
June 20, 1876

To 2nd Lt. H.R. Lemly, 3rd Cavalry
Adjutant Cavalry Command Big Horn & Yellowstone Expedition

Sir:

I respectfully enclose herewith Col. Guy V. Henry's report of the part taken by his Battalion in the action on the 17th inst. As the report in its main points only relates to companies D and F, 3rd Cavalry, I may add that on the morning of the 17th inst, when the order to saddle up was given, companies B and L, 3rd Cavalry (Capt Meinhold and Capt. Vroom's) received orders from you to follow Col Royall, 3rd Cavalry, and we left camp in the order stated above. We formed lines. Col. Royall's escort in front, my company next, Capt Vroom's in my rear, and charged across the open space to the left and front of the camp to a knoll, thence to an adjoining one, opening fire upon the Indians, who seemed to fall back before us. At this moment, I received orders to move with my company (B) rapidly up a ravine to our right, to join Major Noyes 2nd Cavalry at a distance of about 800 yards, and at a place where the canon widens out. I received a very severe fire from Indians on a bluff facing the canon, killing a horse and wounding a man of my company.

On joining Maj. Noyes, I was ordered to take position in his Battalion. While doing so Major Evans 3rd Cavalry ordered me to follow him. I remained with him until the command concentrated and returned to camp. Capt Vroom's company, L 3rd Cavalry was during the entire day under the immediate command of Col Royall. His casualties are as follow

Killed 5 enlisted men
Wounded 3 enlisted men

> Very Respy Yr Obdt Svt.
>> Chas Meinhold
> Captain 3rd
> Cavalry Comdg Batt 3rd Cav.
> Through Col. A.W. Evans, 3rd
> Cav
>> Comdg Batt 3rd Cav.

OFFICIAL REPORT OF CAPTAIN GUY V. HENRY

3rd Cavalry
Camp of South Fork Tongue River Wy
June 20, 1876

2nd Lieut H.R. Lemly, Adjutant Cavalry Command

Sir:

On the morning of the 17th inst my battalion consisting of companies B, D, F and L 3rd Cavalry being in camp on Rose Bud, fire by hostile Indians was heard and the order to saddle up given at once. Major Evans had ordered me to take D and F Companies to the left some 500 yards to form line to prevent the Indians from turning our supposed left: this broke up my battalion. I therefore can only relate the operations of the two companies during the day. (D and F).

Having taken position as ordered, I reconnoitered personally and found Indians some distance to my right on the bluffs. While starting to change my position accordingly, Colonel Royall ordered me to follow him. We took position behind a knoll about a half mile from General Crook's left. While waiting there with his consent, I made such dispositions of my two companies as to prevent the Indians from getting in rear to us, which they were trying to do. The order then came to retire and to connect with General Crook's left. While doing so we were subjected to a very heavy fire from three different points, the Indians having turned our rear as I supposed they would when we retired. They evidentally intending to capture all the lead horses which had been sent to the rear.

It was impossible and unwise under the heavy fire from three directions to keep the men in position they were ordered to retire rapidly with the intention of being rallied under cover. During the retreat we were saved from greater loss by the charge of two infantry companies from General Crook's left, which I personally observed While doing so I was wounded and taken to the rear to have my wound dressed intending to return but the Surgeon forbid me doing so. I may add that upon joining Colonel Royall I found Captain Meinhold and

Vroom Companies over whom I exercised no immediate control, they being under the immediate orders of Colonel Royall. I personally observed however that the officers themselves, Captain Meinhold and Vroom. Lieutenant Simpson and Reynolds were cool and kept their men well in hand and carried out such orders as they received in an efficient manner.

Very respectfully Your Obedient Servant
Guy V Henry 3rd Cavalry Comdg Batt.
By Chas Meinhold
Capt 3rd Cavalry

OFFICIAL REPORT OF
CAPTAIN WILLIAM H. ANDREWS

Co. I, 3rd Cavalry

I Company 3rd U.S. Cavalry
Camp of the Big Horn and Yellowstone Expedition
Goose Creek W.T. June 20, 1876

To Capt Anson Mills Comdg Battn 3rd Cavy.

Sir:

I have the honor to make the following report in regard to the part taken by I Co 3rd Cavy in the affiir of Rosebud Hills on the 17th of June 1876. The Battalion, Capt Mills Cmdg, was moved from the position they were in on the south bank of Rosebud Creek, at about 8 A.M. 17th inst in the following order, A, E, M and I Cos, the first named leading. Taking the trot and passing the creek we dismounted in line in rear of the 2nd Cavalry. In a moment we were again mounted and moved by the flank in the same order at a trot. Three Companies of the Battalion, after gaining a valley, went left front into line, but as I gave the command to my company to comform to this movement, Lt. Col. Royall 3rd Cavy directed me to deploy and carry the ridge on our left which at this time was occupied by the enemy. I did so and then ordered the Company to charge, this deployment being made at the trot. After pushing to the front some considerable distance driving before me and away from the ridge a strong body of the enemy, I halted the company and directed Lieut. Foster to take the 2nd Platoon, numbering eighteen (18) men and "clear those people on the left away" meaning a part of the enemy who threatened to enfilade our line. Charging as foragers under a sharp fire Lieut Foster drove the Indians from three positions in succession and away from the ridges to the left of the ridge along which the balance of the battalion were moving. As soon as Lt Foster had started, I moved forward at a sharp gait with the remainder of the Company, getting at the same time a terribly strong fire from a rocky point on my right. I took possession of this point and held it until ordered back. As long as I held this position I kept the fire in front of me well under. In accordance with orders I sent Private Weaver I Co 3rd Cavy to Lt Foster, who by this time was far in advance of our line, with orders to fall back at once to the Company with the 2nd Platoon, this he did under a very heavy fire from his rear and flanks, marching at a gallop but in good order and having two men and one horse wounded. After some little time I received orders to again fall back, which I did to another point in our rear and received in doing so a heavy fire from the enemy who had occupied the ridge jut abandoned. After remaining here for some time and aiding in checking the enemy who charged our line three times and were each time repulsed with loss, we were ordered to mount and retreat to the high crest upon which the Infantry were posted. In falling back from this position the company suffered its greatest loss, though it had men wounded further to the front. After reaching the crest upon which the Infantry were posted, I was ordered by Lt. Chase, Adj. to Col. Evans to halt until further orders. Subsequently, being so directed by Col Royall, I marched down the crest and brought in the dead of my company, who were brought into the camp that evening and buried. The men of the Company behaved in the most gallant manner throughout the day, and where all did so well it is difficult Matter to particularize, but I desire to mention the very gallant conduct of 1st Serg John Henry; his bearing conduct and bravery I wish specially to commend to the consideration of the General Commanding.

In closing this report I desire to mention the distinguished gallantry of 2nd Lieut. J.E.H. Foster who acted throughtout the whole affair in the most efficient manner, displaying courage and bravery of a very high-order.

Casualties

Killed   Horses
Private Wm W. Allen   Wounded, six (6)
  Do   Eugene Flynn
    Wounded
Sergt Andrew Groesch, Pvts
John Socciborski, James
O'Brien, Francis Smith,
Chas W. Stewart, James
Riley
Force of Company engaged 2 commissioned 46 enlisted.
Capt. Wm H. Andrew
2nd Lieut. J.E.H. Foster
Very Respy Yr Obd Sert

Wm H. Andrews
Capt 3rd Cavy

OFFICIAL REPORT OF CAPTAIN VAN VLIET

Co. C, 3rd Cavalry
Camp on Goose Creek W.T.
June 20th 1876

Major A.W. Evans
Comdg 3rd Cav. Battalion

Major:

In compliance with instructions I have the honor to make the following report of the part taken in action of the 17th inst with hostile Indians. Companies C and G 3rd Cavy, at commencement of action were ordered to gain a commanding ridge in rear of our camp and hold it until further orders. This ridge was gained just in advance of the

Indians who were striving hard for it. These companies remained in this position until about Eleven o'clock when they were withdrawn and joined the main command. No casualties.

I am Major

> Very Respectfully you Obt Servt
> F. Van Vliet
> Capt. 3rd Cav Comdg.

OFFICIAL REPORT OF CAPTAIN ANSON MILLS

Battalion Commander 3rd Cavalry

Head Qrs 1st Batt: Cos A E I and M 3rd Cav.
Big Horn & Yellow Stone Expedition
Goose Creek Wyo June 20th 1876

Lieut. Geo. F. Chase
Adjt Batts 3rd Cav.

Sir:

In compliance with instructions, I have the honor to submit the following report of the part taken by my command in the battle with the hostile Sioux on the 17th inst.

About 8 A.M. while bivouaced in line on the right bank of the Rosebud (between Maynadiers Camp 8 & (where the stream runs from west to east) facing the stream and being the right of the 3rd Cavalry. (The other troops and Indians occupying the opposite bank) skirmishing commenced between the Crows, Snakes and the Sioux. It soon became apparent that we were attacked in force and I received orders from Col Evans to mount, cross the stream and charge and drive the Indians from the opposite hills.

The superior force of the Sioux who now appeared on the hills in large numbers, had driven the Crows and Snakes pell mell into camp but the Battalion 2nd Cav and 9th Inf. had promptly thrown out dismounted skirmishers who held them in check on the first ridge. The Batt. being formed and about ready for the charge, Col. Royall detached Capt Andrews Co I further to the left and he remained so detached during the engagement.

The 3 remaining companies being our extreme right charged the first ridge in our front about 800 yards distant and drove the Indians from it but they immediately formed behind a second some 600 yds. From the first and this also being taken the greater portion of them formed around a large cone shaped mount and when about to move on this I received an order to advance no further but to throw out dismounted skirmishers and hold the position.

The General Commanding soon appeared and informed me that he did not want the engagement pressed any farther then, but that he had ordered all the troops to assemble there when he intended to move the whole command on the village which his information led him to believe was only a short distance below on the stream, that my Batt. should lead pushing as rapidly as the stock would stand it and pay no attention to the assaults of the Sioux as the friendly Indians would flank us (and to charge the village as soon as I got sight of it) 20 men from Co A Lieut. Lawsons, being detailed to accompany the friendly Indians and keep up connections.

I moved out with Co E Capt. Sutorius deployed and soon gained the stream (driving some 30 or 40 Indians from the hills in our former rear and between us and the stream) followed by Noyes' Batt. 2nd Cav. We passed rapidly down the stream, which turns almost due north, for 6 or 7 miles where the bluffs are high, rugged and rocky (Lieut. Bourke Aid to the Comdg Genl and Guide Girard accompanying me with the advance) when I received from Capt. Nickerson the General's order to divert my column to the left and try and gain the rear of some Indians who were making a demonstration in our former front with difficulty we gained the position only to find the Indians had fled and thereupon were ordered into bivouac on the battle field for the night.

My command consisted of:

Co A 3rd Cav Lieut. Lawson Comdg 1 off and 49 men;

Co E 3rd Cav Capt. Sutorius Comg with Lt. Von Leuttwitz 2 off and 54 men.

Co I 3rd Cav Capt Andrews Comdg with Lt Foster 2 off and 46 men

Co M 3rd Cav Lieut Paul Comdg with Lt. Schwatka 2 off and 51 men
Total 7 off: and 200 men

The casualties were Co A 1 horse killed, 1 horse wounded. Co E Pvt Herold wounded. 2 horses wounded. Co I Pvt Allen and Flynn killed. Pvt. Sosciborski, O'Brien, Smith, Riley and Serg. Grosch wounded. Total 2 enlisted men killed and 8 wounded.

All the officers and men behaved with patience, coolness and courage. Messrs Finerty and McMillan, correspondents respectively for the Chicago *Times* and *Inter Ocean* accompanied Co E and A respectively and participated in the engagement throughout.

I submit herewith reports of Company Commanders.

I have the honor to be Very Respectively Your Obed. Servt.
Anson Mills Captain 3rd Cavalry
                                                    Comdg Batt

OFFICIAL REPORT OF LT. JOSEPH LAWSON

Co A 3rd Cavalry
Camp Goose Creek. W.T. June 20, 1876

Captain Anson Mills,
    Commanding First Battalion. Third Cavalry.

I have the honor to submit the following report with reference to the engagement on Rosebud Creek, Montana Territory, June 17, 1876. Company A participated occupying through the first charge the left center and during the Second charge the left. It was while A Company was on the left of the skirmish line that Sergeant John H. Van Moll acted courageously in advancing to the enemies lines, supported only by a few friendly Indian allies, by whom he was rescued and brought to our lines. One horse was killed, and one wounded in action. No casualties among the men occurred. Private Leonard acted in a commendable manner during the engagement. The company non-commissioned officers and privates deserve credit for their efficiency and bravery.

I am Sir Very Respectfully Your Obedient Servant

Joseph Lawson
1st Lieut. 3rd Cavalry
Commanding Co A

OFFICIAL REPORT OF LT. AUGUSTUS C. PAUL

Co M 3rd Cavalry

Camp on Goose Creek Wyo T.
June 20th, 1876

Capt Anson Mills 3rd Cavly
Commanding 1st Battalion Captain

I have the honor to report that M Company 3rd Cavalry participated in the engagement against the Sioux Indians June 17th near the head of the Rosebud as a part of the 1st Battalion. In the charges both mounted and dismounted the Company behaved handsomely. Sec Lieut Frederick Schwatka throughout the entire fight acted very courageously. Trumpeter Snow while in the extreme advance in the charge made by the 1st Battalion was badly wounded through the right and left arm.

I have the honor to be very respectfully Your Obedient servant.

August C. Paul
1st Lieut. 3rd Cavy
Comdg Co M 3rd Cavalry.

Notes

Chapter 1

[1] "Report of Colonel Joseph J. Reynolds" on the Battle of Powder River. Original in National Archives, copy contained in J.W. Vaughn, *The Reynolds Campaign on Powder River,* p. 211. The most definitive treatment of the Powder River battle is in J.W. Vaughn. John S. Gray, *Centennial Campaign,* devotes a chapter to the fight which is an excellent condensation of Vaughn's work. Another account less authoratative, but still good is Fred Werner, *The Soldiers are Coming.*

[2] John C. Bourke, *On the Border with Crook,* p. 279.

[3] Joe De Barthe, *The Life and Adventures of Frank Grouard,* p. 101; Vaughn, *Reynolds Campaign,* pp. 58-59.

[4] Neil C. Mangum, "The Battle on Powder River," in *Hoofprints, Yellowstone Corral of the Westerners.* Vol. 13 No. 1 (Spring-Summer 1983); Vaughn, *Reynolds Campaign,* p. 60.

[5] Mangum, p. 18; Vaughn, *Reynolds Campaign, p. 61.*

[6] Vaughn, *Reynolds Campaign, p. 208. "Report of Colonel Reynolds".*

[7] *Ibid.*

[8] *Ibid.,* p. 100; Gray, *Centennial Campaign,* p. 56; Frank Grouard also claimed that the village was Crazy Horse's, De Barthe, *Frank Grouard,* p. 98.

[9] Mari Sandoz, *Crazy Horse, the Strange Man of the Oglalas,* p. 304; Thomas B. Marquis, *Wooden Leg: A Warrior Who fought Custer,* p. 167.

[10] Vaughn, *Reynolds Campaign,* p. 92 Court-Martial Proceedings of Colonel Joseph J. Reynolds, Custer Battlefield Historical Files.

[11] For a summary of this portion of the battle see "Official Report of Colonel Joseph J. Reynolds" contained in Vaughn, *Reynolds Campaign,* pp 209-210.

[12] *Ibid., pp. 101-103.*

[13] "Official Report of Captain Anson B. Mills" on the Battle of Powder River. p. 218, copy contained in Vaughn, *Reynolds Campaign.*

[14] "Official Report of Captain Henry Noyes" on the Battle of Powder River, p. 223, copy contained in Vaughn, *Reynolds Campaign.*

[15] *Ibid.*

[16] Bourke, *On the Border with Crook,* p. 279.

[17] *Ibid.*

[18] "Official Report of Colonel Reynolds," pp. 211-12, contained in Vaughn, *Reynolds Campaign.*

[19] Joseph C. Porter, *Paper Medicine Man John Gregory Bourke and His American West,* quoted in, p. 36.

[20] Paul L. Hedren, *Fort Laramie in 1876,* p. 75.

[21] Vaughn, *Reynolds Campaign,* p. 168.

Chapter 2

[1] Paul A. Hutton, *Phil Sheridan and His Army,* p. 116.

[2] Martin F. Schmitt, *General George Crook His Autobiography,* pp. xxii-xxiii.

[3] *Ibid.,* p. xxii.

[4] Ezra Warner, *Generals In Blue,* p. 102; George W. Cullum, *Biographical Register of the Officers and Graduates of the U.S. Military Academy at West Point,* p. 329; Francis B. Heitman, *Historical Register and Dictionary of the United States Army from its Organization, September 29, 1789, to March 2, 1902,* p. 340

[5] Schmitt, *Crook Autobiography,* p. xxiii.

[6] Jerome A. Greene, *Slim Buttes, 1876,* p. 15. Schmitt, *Crook Autobiography,* p. 40.

[7] Schmitt, *Crook Autobiography,* fn. pp. 90-91; Whitelaw Reid, *Ohio in the War,* p. 235; U.S. War Department, *The War of the Rebellion; a Compilation of the Official Records of the Union and Confederate Armies,* pp. 803-808, Ser. I, Vol. XII.

[8] Frederick H. Dyer, *A Compendium of the War of the Rebellion,* III Vol., Vol. I, p. 338

[9] Schmitt, *Crook Autobiography,* p. 101.

[10] *Ibid.* p. 92.

[11] *Ibid.* p. 93.

[12] *Ibid.* p. 95.

[13] *Ibid.* p. 101.

[14] *Ibid.* p. 114.

[15] *Ibid.* p. 115.

[16] *Battles and Leaders,* 4 Vol., edited by Robert U. Johnson and Clarence C. Buell, Vol. IV, p. 477 and 488.

[17] Schmitt, *Crook Autobiography*, pp. 116-121. Excellent accounts of Hunter's abortive endeavor to take Lynchburg can be found in *Battles and Leaders*, Vol IV and Edward J. Stackpole, *Sheridan in the Shenandoah*.

[18] Hutton, *Phill Sheridan and His Army*, p. 124.

[19] *Ibid., p. 125.*

[20] *Ibid., p. 125; quoted in Schmitt, Crook Autobiography*, p. 134.

[21] Hutton, *Phil Sheridan and His Army*, p. 126.

[22] Warner, *Generals in Blue*, p. 103.

[23] Schmitt, *Crook Autobiography*, pp. 135-136.

[24] Hutton, *Phil Sheridan and His Army*, p. 126.

[25] Paul L. Hedren, *Fort Laramie in 1876*, p. 106, quoted in; *Cheyenne Daily Leader*, May 24, 1876.

[26] Hutton, *Phil Sheridan and His Army*, p. 126.

[27] Robert M. Utley, *Custer Battlefield Handbook*, p. 17; Edgar I. Stewart, *Custer's Luck*, pp. 84-85.

[28] Robert M. Utley, *Frontier Regulars*, p. 258.

[29] *Ibid., p. 260.*

[30] *Ibid., p. 261.*

Chapter 3

[1] Hedren, *Fort Laramie in 1876*, p. 84.

[2] *Ibid., p. 85.*

[3] *Ibid., p. 96.*

[4] *Ibid., p. 101.*

[5] Bourke, *On the Border with Crook*, p. 287.

[6] *New York Herald*, June 9, 1876; quoted in James C. Olson, *Red Cloud and the Sioux Problem*, p. 218.

[7] Hedren, *Fort Laramie in 1876*, p. 101; Bourke, *On the Border with Crook*, p. 286-87.

[8] Hedren, *Fort Laramie in 1876*, p. 103.

[9] Bourke, *On the Border with Crook*, p. 289.

[10] *Ibid., pp. 289-290.*

[11] For more information on Bourke see *Joseph C. Porter, John Gregory Bourke and His American West;* William G. Belle, *John Gregory Bourke: A Soldier-Scientist on the Frontier;* and John A. Turcheneske, Jr., "John G. Bourke: Troubled Scientist," *Journal of Arizona History* 20 (Autumn, 1979): 323-44. Bourke also faithfully maintained a diary from 1869-1896. With the exception of the entries for 1869-1872, which apparently have become lost, the surviving

volumes have been preserved. They are now housed at the Library of the United States Military Academy, West Point, New York.

[12] John S. Gray, *Centennial Campaign*, p. 111; J.W. Vaughn, *Indians Fights*, p. 120.

[13] Mark H. Brown, *Plainsmen of the Yellowstone*, p. 257.

[14] Greene, *Slim Buttes*, p. 5.

[15] *Ibid.*, pp. 23-24; For a complete description of the campaign dress, accouterments, and horse gear, see James S. Hutchins, *Boots and Saddles at the Little Bighorn*.

[16] Records of U.S. Army Continental Commands, 1821-1930, entry 1342, Record Group 393, National Archives, Washington, D.C.

[17] Ray Meketa, "Diary May 29th to October 30th, G.L. Luhn 4th Infantry." No date; (Transcribed from Luhn Diary now preserved in Coe Library, University of Wyoming, Laramie); See also James H. Nottage, eds., "The Big Horn and Yellowstone Expedition of 1876 As Seen Through the Letters of Captain Gerhard Luke Luhn," *Annals of Wyoming*, 45 (Spring 1973)

[18] John F. Finerty, *War-Path ad Bivouac*, p. 57.

[19] Bourke, *Diary* quoted in J.W. Vaughn, With Crook, p. 12.

[20] Vaughn, *With Crook*, p. 12.

[21] Finerty, *War-Path and Bivouac*, p. 58.

[22] Ray Meketa, "Diary of G.L. Luhn" (transcribed)

[23] "Narrative of Big Horn and Yellowstone Expedition June 1 to June 21, 1876, By A. Harstuff, Assistant Surgeon, U.S.A. Medical Dirctory of Expedition," Vaughn Papers, Coe Library, University of Wyoming, Laramie; *Chicago Tribune*, July 5, 1876.

[24] Finerty, *War-Path and Bivouac*, p. 57.

[25] Gray, *Centennial Campaign*, p. 112.

[26] Finerty, *War-Path and Bivouac*, p. 71.

[27] Anson Mills, *My Story*, pp. 397-398; Merrill J. Mattes, *Indians, Infants, and Infantry*, p. 216, indicates this episode occurred after Crook's command reached Goose Creek, June 12-14.

[28] Gray, *Centennial Campaign*, p. 113.

[29] *Ibid.*

[30] Finerty, *War-Path and Bivouac*, pp. 7-71.

[31] *Ibid.*, p. 75.

[32] Finerty, *War-Path and Bivouac*, p. 77.

[33] *Ibid.*, pp. 78-79.

[34] Ray Meketa, "Diary of G.L. Luhn" (transcribed); Merril J. Mattes, *Indians, Infants and Infantry*, p. 216, indicates miners arrived the same evening. However, he states all 65 miners, not just the two as Luhn suggests,

came in. Finerty, *War-Path and Bivouac,* p. 79 and Bourke, *On the Border with Crook,* p. 293, states the arrival of two miners occurred on June 4, at the Clear Creek encampment; Mark Brown, *Plainsmen of the Yellowstone,* p. 260, gives June 3, at Crazy Woman Creek, as the date and site of the pair of miners joining the command.

[35] Vaughn, *With Crook at the Rosebud,* p. 16.

[36] Cynthia J. Capron, *The Indian Border War of 1876 from Letters of Lieutenant Thaddeus Capron,* p. 10, copy on file at Fort Laramie National Monument, Fort Laramie, Wyoming, reprinted from the *Journal of the Illinois State Historical Society,* 1921.

[37] Cynthia J. Capron, *Letters of Lieutenant Thaddeus Capron,* p. 10.

[38] Ray Meketa, "Diary of G.L. Luhn" (transcribed) diary entry for June 6.

[39] Gray, *Centennial Campaign,* p. 113.

[40] *Ibid;* Thomas B. Marquis, *Wooden Leg A Warrior Who Fought Custer,* pp. 193-194.

[41] James H. Nottage, ed., "The Big Horn and Yellowstone Expedition of 1876" (Letters of Captain Gerhard L. Luhn), letter of June 11, *Annals of Wyoming,* Spring, 1973, p. 31.

[42] Nottage, "Luhn Letters," June 11; Gray, *Centennial Campaign,* p. 114.

[43] Meketa, "Diary of G.L. Luhn" (transcribed) diary entry for June 7.

[44] Finerty, *War-Path and Bivouac,* p. 187; Bourke, *On the Border with Crook,* pp. 294-95.

[45] Bourke, *On the Border with Crook,* pp. 294-95; Bourke Diary 4:356.

[46] *Chicago Tribune,* July 5, 1876; *Alta California,* July 6, 1876.

[47] Finerty, *War-Path and Bivouac,* p. 295.

[48] Finerty, *War-Path and Bivouac,* p. 190; *New York Herald,* June 6, 1876.

[49] *New York Herald,* June 16, 1876.

[50] Ray Meketa, "Diary of G.L. Luhn" (transcribed) diary entry for June 8.

[51] Bourke, *On the Border with Crook,* p. 295.

[52] Cynthia J. Capron, *Letters of Lieutenant Thaddeus Capron,* p. 12.

[53] *Ibid.*

[54] Finerty, *War-Path and Bivouac,* p. 93.

[55] *Ibid.,* pp. 95-96; "Luhn Letters," James H. Nottage ed., *Annals of Wyoming* 45, Spring 1973, p. 32.

[56] "Luhn Letters," James H. Nottage, ed., *Annals of Wyoming* 45, Spring 1973, p. 32.

[57] *New York Herald,* June 16, 1876.

[58] *Army and Navy Journal,* June 24, 1876.

[59] *New York Herald,* June 16, 1876.

[60] Mattes, *Indians, Infants, and Infantry,* p. 216.
[61] George B. Grinnell, *Fighting Cheyennes,* p. 329.
[62] *Chicago Tribune,* July 5, 1876.

Chapter 4

[1] Records of United States Army Continental Commands, 1821-1930, entry 1243, Record Group 393, National Archives, Washington, D.C., dispatch from Crook to Sheridan, June 11, 1876.
[2] "Luhn Letters," James H. Nottage ed., *Annals of Wyoming,* 45, Spring 1973, p. 33.
[3] Bourke, *On the Border with Crook,* p. 298.
[4] Gray, *Centennial Campaign,* p. 114.
[5] Ray Meketa, *Marching With General Crook,* the diary of Lieutenant Thadeus Hurlbut Capron Company C, Ninth Infantry, Ray Meketa ed., p. 16.
[6] Mattes, *Indians, Infants, and Infantry,* p. 217.
[7] De Barthe, *The Life and Adventures of Frank Grouard,* p. 301.
[8] For the best account of the Sioux raid on the Crow pony herd see Gray, *Centennial Campaign,* p. 77. Edgar Stewart, *Custer's Luck,* pp. 140-141.
[9] De Barthe, *The Life and Adventures of Frank Grouard,* p. 124.
[10] Bourke, *On the Border with Crook,* pp. 301-302.
[11] *Ibid.*
[12] Brown, *Plainsmen of the Yellowstone,* p. 262.
[13] Bourke, *On the Border with Crook,* p. 303.
[14] Bourke Diary 5:384 in Porter, *Paper Medicine Man,* p. 40; Bourke, *On the Border with Crook,* p. 305.
[15] Bourke, *On the Border with Crook,* pp. 302-303. Bourke Diary 5:384-396.
[16] Finerty, *War-Path and Bivouac,* p. 105.
[17] Vaughn, *With Crook at the Rosebud,* p. 26.
[18] De Barthe, *The Life and Adventures of Frank Grouard,* p. 123.
[19] "Narrative of Big Horn and Yellowstone Expedition June 1 to June 21, 1876, by A. Hartsuff, Assistant Surgeon, U.S.A. Medical Director of Expedition." in Vaughn Papers, Coe Library, University of Wyoming, Laramie.
[20] Vaughn, *With Crook at the Rosebud,* p. 31.

Chapter 5

[1] Bourke, *On the Border with Crook,* p. 307; Brown, *The Plainsmen of the Yellowstone,* p. 263.
[2] *New York Herald,* July 6, 1876.

3 Vaughn, *Indian Fights: New Facts on Seven Encounters,* p. 127.

4 "Capron Diary" Ray Meketa ed., p. 13.

5 John Stands in Timber and Margot Liberty, *Cheyenne Memories,* pp. 182-183.

6 Peter J. Powell, *Sweet Medicine,* p. 101

7 De Barthe, *The Life and Adventures of Frank Grouard,* p. 124.

8 The question of Indian numbers at the Battle of the Rosebud like most other soldier-Indian confrontations in the West produces a wide range. Gray, *Centennial Campaign,* p. 120, provides a good argument for the lowest figure seen in print, 750. At the other end of the spectrum is Crazy Horse's statement in *South Dakota Historical Collections* Vol. 6, p. 228, which states 6000 Indians were at the fight, 1500 in battle and 4500 waiting in concealment. Eyewitnesses to the fight who should perhaps be the best critics give wide ranging figures too. Averaging them out brings the warrior count to about 1000-1500.

9 According to people at the Battle of the Rosebud the number of warriors present range from 1500-2500. Finerty, *War-Path and Bivouac,* and the *New York Herald,* July 24, 1876, place the warrior force at 2500. Finerty states his figure is based on what Crook told him, p. 130. Captain Anson Mills in *My Story,* p. 405 is in agreement with Crook. Edgar Stewart, *Custer's Luck,* p. 200, puts the Indian total at 1000-1500; Captain G.L. Luhn in his June 19th letter puts the figure at 1500; Stanley Vestal in *Sitting Bull;* p. 153, estimates the warrior force at less than 1000.

10 Finerty, *War-Path and Bivouac,* pp. 120-121.

11 Mills, *My Story,* p. 400.

12 *Ibid.*

13 Bourke, *On the Border with Crook,* p. 310; Bourke Diary 5:404.

14 Vaughn, *With Crook at the Rosebud,* p. 135.

15 Bourke Diary 5:404; Porter, *Paper Medicine Mn,* p. 42.

16 Bourke Diary 5:404.

Chapter 6

1 Finerty, *War-Path and Bivouac,* p. 126.

2 Cyrus Townsend Brady, *Indian Fights and Fighters,* p. 204.

3 Vaughn, *With Crook at the Rosebud,* p. 48.

4 *Ibid.,* p.49.

5 There is considerable confusion regarding the placement of the various commands at the battle's outset. Mills, *My Story,* p. 403, puts Mills and Noyes on the right bank followed by Henry, Van Vliet, and the Infantry on

the left bank. Mills' map of troop disposition is repeated in Brady, *Indian Fights and Fighters*, p. 197; Finerty, *War-Path and Bivouac*, p. 125. Unfortunately, Mills location is wrong. The Third Cavalry had been marching entirely upon the right bank, Official Report of Major Andrew Evans; Captain H.R. Lemly, "The Fight on the Rosebud" in *Valor and Arms*, p. 8; Chicago *Tribune*, July 5, 1876. Vaughn, *With Crook at the Rosebud*, p. 49, has a slightly different version placing Mills and Henry on the right and Noyes, Van Vliet, and Chamber's infantry on the left.

[6] Vaughn, *New Facts*, p. 129.

[7] Porter, *Paper-Medicine*, p. 42.

[8] Finerty, *War-Path and Bivouac*, p. 126.

[9] Powell, *Sweet Medicine*, p. 103.

[10] Vaughn, *With Crook at the Rosebud*, p. 50.

[11] *Ibid.*

[12] Marquis, *Wooden Legs*, p. 200.

[13] Sandoz, *Crazy Horse*, p. 318.

[14] Vaughn, *New Facts*, pp. 130-131.

[15] *Ibid.*, p. 130.

[16] Official Report of Captain Frederick Van Vliet.

[17] Official Report of Captain Guy V. Henry.

[18] Brown, *Plainsmen of the Yellowstone*, p. 267; The other wounded Crow was Fox-Just-Coming-Over-Hill, later renamed Old Coyote, Vaughn, *New Facts*, p. 131.

[19] Vaughn, *New Facts*, p. 131; De Barthe, *The Life and Adventures of Frank Grouard*, p. 125.

[20] Official Report of Major Alexander Chambers.

[21] Meketa, "Capron Diary," p. 19.

[22] Nickerson, Azor H., *Major General George Crook and the Indians*, pp. 26-27, U.S. Army Military History Institute, Carlisle Barracks, Pa.; Vaughn, *With Crook at the Rosebud*, p. 101.

[23] Official Report of Captain Henry Noyes; Vaughn, *With Crook at the Rosebud*, p. 51.

[24] Vaughn, *With Crook at the Rosebud*, p. 90.

[25] *Ibid.*, p.52.

[26] Official Report of Captain Guy V. Henry.

[27] Grinnell, *Fighting Cheyennes*, p. 321; Mattes, *Indians, Infants, and Infantry*, p. 219.

[28] Sandoz, *Crazy Horse*, p. 319.

[29] Stands in Timber, *Cheyenne Memories*, p. 189; Buffalo-Calf-Road-Woman

was not through as a woman warrior. At Little Bighorn she fought beside her husband Black Coyote, Marquis, *Cheyennes of Montana,* p. 67. She died at Fort Keogh several years after the battle, Stanley Vestal, *Warpath and Council Fire,* pp. 224-25; Marquis, *Cheyennes of Montana,* p. 68, fn.

[30] Lemly, "The Fight on the Rosebud," *Valor and Arms,* pp. 9-10.

Chapter 7

[1] Mills, *My Story,* p. 401.
[2] Finerty, *War-Path and Bivouac,* p. 127.
[3] Vaughn, *With Crook at the Rosebud,* p. 72.
[4] Mills, *My Story,* p. 402.
[5] Vaughn, *With Crook at the Rosebud,* p. 53.
[6] *Ibid.,* p. 53.
[7] Official Report of Captain Anson Mills.
[8] *Ibid.*
[9] Official Report of Captain Henry Noyes.
[10] Official Report of Captain Andrew S. Burt.
[11] *Ibid.;* the wounded men consisted of Privates James Devine, Richard Flynn, and John Terry, Company D Fourth Infantry, Vaughn, *With Crook at the Rosebud,* p. 95; there was one wounded cavalryman, Corporal Thomas Meagher, Company I Second Cavalry, Bourke Diary 5:406.

Chapter 8

[1] Official Report of Major Andrew Evans.
[2] *New York Herald,* July 6, 1876.
[3] Official Report of Captain William Andrews.
[4] *New York Herald,* July 6, 1876.
[5] Official Report of William Andrews.
[6] *Ibid.*
[7] Lemly, "The Fight on the Rosebud," *Valor and Arms,* p. 8.
[8] Vaughn, *With Crook at the Rosebud,* p. 55.
[9] *New York Herald,* July 6, 1876.
[10] Official Report of Lieutenant Colonel William B. Royall.
[11] *Ibid.*
[12] *New York Herald,* July 6, 1876.
[13] Official Report of Captain Charles Meinhold.
[14] "Return of Killed, Wounded and missing of the troops serving under command Brig. Genl. Crook in the action with hostile Sioux on Rosebud

River June 17, 1876," copy in Vaughn Papers, Coe library, U. of Wyoming.

[15] Vaughn, *New Facts,* p. 134.

[16] Finerty, *War-Path and Bivouac,* p. 135.

[17] *Ibid.*

[18] Gray, *Centennial Campaign,* p. 122.

[19] *Ibid.*

[20] Vaughn, *With Crook at the Rosebud,* p. 113.

[21] Official Report of Captain Guy V. Henry.

[22] Bourke, *On the Border with Crook,* p. 314.

[23] Official Report of Captain Frederick Van Vliet; Reporter Reuben Davenport writing for the *New York Herald,* July 6, 1876, indicates that Lt. Foster and his squad was the force that went down to the mouth of Kollmar to intercept the Indians. Davenport is in error. Foster's attack on the Sioux had occurred after separating from Andrews, fully a mile west. See Official Report of Lt. James Foster; Finerty, *War-Path and Bivouac,* p. 144.

[24] Bourke, *On the Border with Crook,* p. 314.

[25] Bourke Diary 5:407.

[26] Bourke Diary 5:408.

[27] Bourke Diary 5:408; Lt. Augustus Paul in his Offical Report said Snow was shot through right and left arm.

[28] Bourke Diary 5:408.

[29] Porter, *Paper Medicine Man,* p. 44; Finerty, *War-Path and Bivouac,* p. 133.

[30] Finerty, *War-Path and Bivouac,* p. 133.

[31] Porter, *Paper Medicine Man,* p. 44.

[32] Bourke, *On the Border with Crook,* p. 313.

[33] Meketa, "Capron Diary," p. 20.

[34] Official Report of Captain Avery Cain.

[35] Official Report of Captain Samuel Munson.

[36] Official Report of Captain Frederick Van Vliet.

[37] *Rocky Mountain News,* July 4, 1876, quoted in Oliver Knight, *Following the Indian Wars,* p. 188.

[38] Lemly, "The Fight on the Rosebud," *Valor and Arms,* p. 9.

[39] *Ibid.*

[40] Vaughn, *New Facts,* p. 141.

[41] Powell, *Sweet Medicine,* p. 104; John Stands in Timber, *Cheyenne Memories,* pp. 187-188.

[42] Vaughn, *With Crook at the Rosebud,* p. 113.

[43] *Ibid.,* p. 114.

[44] Lemly, "The Fight on the Rosebud, *Valor and Arms,* p. 9; *New York*

Herald, July 6, 1876.

[45] James Willert, *Little Big Horn Diary,* p. 168.

[46] Official Report of Lieutenant Colonel William B. Royall.

[47] *New York Herald,* July 6, 1876.

[48] Muster Roll, Company L Third U.S. Cavalry.

[49] Vaughn, *With Crook at the Rosebud,* p. 114.

[50] *Army-Navy Journal,* July 22, 1876; copy in John Carroll, *The Battle of the Rosebud Plus Three.*

[51] *Ibid.*

[52] W.F. Beyer and O.F. Keydel, editors, *Deeds of Valor,* pp. 208-210. Shingle for his decisive action in the face of the enemy was cited with bravery and earned the coveted Medal of Honor for action at Rosebud Creek.

[53] *New York Daily Graphic,* July 13, 19'876.

[54] *Ibid.,* Carroll, *Battle of the Rosebud Plus Three,* p. 52.

[55] "Winners of the West," , May 30, 1934.

[56] *Ibid.*

[57] *New York Herald,* July 6, 1876.

[58] *Army-Navy Journal,* July 22, 1876.

[59] Accounts of who rescued Henry conflict and cannot easily be reconciled. De Barthe, *The Life and Adventures of Frank Grouard,* p. 127, says it was Yute John who rescued Henry. Virginia Trenhom and Maurine Carley, *The Shoshones Sentinels of the Rockies,* p. 251, credits a Shoshone by the name of Tigee. Reporter Davenport in the July 6, 1876, *New York Herald,* claims that two soldiers saved Henry. Adjutant Lemly in his "Fight on the Rosebud" in *Valor and Arms,* p. 9, says it was two Crows.

[60] Trenhom and Carley, *The Shoshones Sentinels of the Rockies,* p. 251.

[61] Frank Linderman, *Plenty Coups, Chief of the Crows,* p. 166.

[62] "Winners of the West," May 30, 1934.

[63] *New York Daily Graphic,* July 13, 1876.

[64] Brady, *Indian Fights and Fighters,* p. 207.

[65] *New York Herald,* July 6, 1876.

[66] *New York Daily Graphic,* July 13, 1876.

[67] *New York Herald,* July 6, 1876.

[68] Vaughn, *With Crook at the Rosebud,* p. 115.

[69] Gray, *Centennial Campaign,* p. 122.

[70] Official Report of Captain Andrew S. Burt; Mattes, *Indians, Infants, and Infantry,* p. 219.

[71] Official Report of Captain Andrew S. Burt.

[72] Official Report of Captain Guy V. Henry.

[73] Luhn Letter, July 23, 1876.

[74] Mattes, *Indians, Infants, and Infantry,* p. 219.

[75] Bourke Diary 5:409.

[76] Lemly, "The Fight on the Rosebud," *Valor and Arms,* p. 9.

[77] Henry Daly, *American Legion Magazine,* April, 1927, quoted in Vaughn, *With Crook at the Rosebud,* pp. 109-111.

Chapter 9

[1] De Barthe, *The Life and Adventures of Frank Grouard,* p. 134.

[2] Official Report of Captain Anson Mills.

[3] De Barthe, *The Life and Adventures of Frank Grouard,* p. 135.

[4] Knight, *Following the Indian Wars,* p. 18.

[5] De Barthe, *The Life and Adventures of Frank Grouard,* p. 135; Lt. Lemly states the reason for Mills' recall was out of fear for the battalion's safety and not so much to reinforce Crook, Lemly, "The Fight on the Rosebud," *Valor and Arms,* p. 9.

[6] Mills, *My Story,* p. 404.

[7] *Ibid.*

[8] *Ibid.*

[9] *Ibid.*

[10] Lemly, "The Fight on the Rosebud," *Valor and Arms,* p. 10.

[11] Vaughn, *With Crook at the Rosebud,* p. 65.

[12] Lemly, "The Fight on the Rosebud," *Valor and Arms,* p. 10.

[13] *Ibid.*

[14] De Barthe, *The Life and Adventures of Frank Grouard,* p. 128.

[15] Finerty, *War-Path and Bivouac,* pp. 90-91.

[16] Bourke, *On the Border with Crook,* p. 315.

[17] Mills, *My Story,* p. 405.

[18] Grinnell, *Fighting Cheyennes,* p. 344.

[19] Powell, *Sweet Medicine* and John Stands in Timber, *Cheyenne Memories.*

[20] On the other hand Maria Sandoz, *Crazy Horse,* p. 320, states Crazy Horse did not attempt to decoy soldiers in a well laid trap.

[21] Vestal, *Warpath and Council Fire,* p. 229.

[22] "Winners of the West," May 30, 1934.

[23] Lemly, "The Fight on the Rosebud," *Valor and Arms,* p. 10.

[24] "Return of Killed, Wounded and missing of the troops serving under command Brig Genl. Geo. Crook in the action with hostile Sioux on Rosebud River June 17, 1876," copy in Vaughn Papers, Coe Library, U. of Wyoming. One of the most controversial aspects of the Battle of the Rosebud

is centered around the number of casualties. It need not be controversial yet historians have attempted to imply that Crook may have been covering up by reducing the number of killed and wounded. Under scrutinization the conspiracy accusation does not hold up. Crook's return of the killed and wounded when compared to the official reports generated by the company officers matches closely. In fact the killed coincide exactly. What discrepencies encountered is among the wounded. Lt. Lemly, "The Fight on the Rosebud," lists 10 killed, Captain Luhn wrote 9 killed, 20 wounded; Bourke in his diary reported 57 casualties of all types; the most outrageous accounting of casualties comes from Grouard who recounted 28 killed and 56 wounded.

25 Official Report of General George Crook; Crazy Horse's account of the battle contained in "Crazy Horse's Story of Custer Battle" in South Dakota Historical Collection, Vol. 6, p. 278, places the total casualties of Sioux and Cheyenne at 36 killed and 63 wounded.

26 *South Dakota Historical Collection*, p. 278.

27 Finerty, *War-Path and Bivouac*, p. 141.

28 Official Report of Asst. Surgeon A.H. Hartsuff to Medical Director of Department of Platte, Omaha Neb., June 20, 1876, contained in Vaughn Papers, Coe Library, U. of Wyoming.

29 *Hardin Tribune-Herald*, January 20, 1933, "James Forristell, Aged Business Man of Bozeman, was a Cavalryman During Frontier Days."

30 "Winners of the West," October 30, 1933; *Army-Navy Journal*, July 22, 1876, indicates the dead were placed in one large grave along the bank of the Rosebud. John G. Neihardt, *Black Elk Speaks*, p. 104, reports the Indians returned to the battlefield on the 18th and found graves of soldiers at the site of their encampment; this account is collaborated by Finerty, *War-Path and Bivouac*, p. 146.

31 Lemly, "The Fight on the Rosebud," *Valor and Arms*, p. PY.

32 *Ibid.*

33 *New York Herald*, July 6, 1876.

Chapter 10

1 Lemly, "The Fight on the Rosebud," *Valor and Arms*, p. 11.

2 *New York Herald*, July 6, 1876. Bourke, *On the Border with Crook*, p. 318.

3 Bourke, *On the Border With Crook*, p. 317.

4 Lemly, "The Fight on the Rosebud," *Valor and Arms*, p. 11.

5 Nickerson MS, p. 29.

6 Lemly, "The Fight on the Rosebud," *Valor and Arms*, p. 11.

7 Willert, *Little Big Horn Diary*, p. 178.

[8] Official Report of General George Crook.

[9] National Archives, Entry 1342, RG 393, Records of U.S. Army Continental Commands, 1821-1930.

[10] Secretary of War, Annual Report, 1876, p. 500; House of Rep., Ex. Doc. No. 1, Pt. 2, 44th Congress, 2nd Session, Report of the Sec. of War, Report of the General of the Army.

[11] Schmitt, *General George Crook His Autobiography,* p. 195.

[12] Secretary of War, Annual Report, 1876, p. 440.

[13] Schmitt, *General George Crook,* p. 196.

[14] Porter, *Paper Medicine Man,* p. 45.

[15] *Ibid.,* p. 46

[16] *Ibid.*

[17] *Ibid.,* pp. 46-47

[18] *New York Herald,* June 27, 1876.

[19] *New York Herald,* July 6, 1876.

[20] *Ibid.*

Chapter 11

[1] Virginia Johnson, *The Unregimented General A Biography of Nelson A. Miles, p. 90-91; Brian Pohanka, editor, Nelson A. Miles,* Miles thought Crook vacillatory and unreliable. Crook was not without his support. Sherman thought highly of Crook's military skills. He considered him foremost of his western Indians commanders, S.L.A. Marshall, *Crimsoned Prairie,* pp. 122-123.

[2] Robert G. Athearn, *William Tecumseh Sherman and the Settlement of West,* p. 314.

[3] Telegraphic Report of General Crook, written June 19, 1876, received June 23, 1876.

Chapter 12

[1] Letter from Walter M. Camp to W.D. Fisher, January 12, 1920, Custer Battlefield National Monument, Walter M. Camp Papers.

[2] *Winners of the West,* June 30, 1934.

Bibliography

Manuscripts

Carlisle Barracks, Pennsylvania. United States Army Military History Institute. Crook-Kennon Collection.

Crow Agency, Montana. Custer Battlefield National Monument

———. Reynolds Court-Martial.

———. Walter M. Camp Papers.

———. Historical Photographs File.

Douglas, Alaska. Ray Meketa. "Diary of Gerhard Luhn" (transcript).

Helena, Montana. Neil Mangum. "Rosebud Battlefield Historic Base Data Study".

Laramie, Wyoming. University of Wyoming ', Coe Library. J.W. Vaughn Papers.

Washington, D.C. National Archives. Record Group 393. Records of the United States Continental Commands.

West Point, United States Military Academy Library. John G. Bourke Diaries.

Goverment Publications

Hedren, Paul L. *Fort Laramie in 1876: Chronicle of A Post At War.* National Park Service, 1986.

Heitman, Francis B. compiler. *Historical Register and Dictionary of the United States Army, from its Organization, September 29, 1789, to March 2, 1903.* 2 vols. Washington, D.C.: Government Printing Office, 1903.

Report of the Secretary of War, 1876. Washington, D.C.: Government Printing Office, 1876.

Taylor, Margee, "Rosebud Battle Reconstruction Overlays". Billings: Bureau of Land Management, n.d.

Utley, Robert M. *Custer Battlefield Handbook.* Washington, D.C. Goverment Printing Office, 1969.

War Department. *The War of the Rebellion: A Compilation of the Official Records of the Union and Confederate Armies.* Washington, D.C.: U.S. Government Printing Office, 1880-1891.

Articles

Daly, Henry W. *American Legion Magazine.* April, 1927.

Lemly, Captain H.R. "The Fight on the Rosebud," *Valor and Arms,* (Summer 1975).

Mangum, Neil C. "The Battle on Powder River." *Hoofprints, Yellowstone Corral of the Westerners.* 13 (Spring-Summer 1983).

Nottage, James H. ed. "The Big Horn and Yellowstone Expedition of 1876 as Seen Through the Letters of Captain Gerhard Lake Luhn." *Annals of Wyoming* 45 Spring 1973.

South Dakota Historical Collection. "Crazy Horse's Story of Custer Battlefield," Vol. 6, 1912.

Newspapers

Army and Navy Journal
Cheyenne Daily Leader
Chicago Tribune
Denver Rocky Mountain News
Hardin Tribune-Herald
New York Daily Graphic
New York Herald
San Francisco Alta California
Winners of the West

Books

Athearn, Robert G. *William Tecumseh Sherman and the Settlement of the West.* Norman: University of Oklahoma Press, 1956.

Beyer, W.F. and O.F. Keydel, editors. *Deeds of Valor,* 2 Volumes. Detroit, 1906.

Bourke, *On the Border with Crook,* New York: Charles Scribner's Sons, 1891.

Brady, Cyrus Townsend. *Indian Fights and Fighters.* Lincoln: University of Nebraska Press, 1972.

Brown, Mark H. *The Plainsmen of the Yellowstone: A History of the Yellowstone*

Basin. New York: G.P. Putnam's Sons, 1961.

Capron, Cynthia J. "The Indian Border War of 1876." *Journal of the Illinois State Historical Society* 13 (January, 1921) Reprint.

Capron, Lt. Thaddeus H. "Marching With General Crook," Ray Meketa, editor. Douglas, Alaska: Cheechako Press, 1983.

Carroll, John M. *The Battle of the Rosebud Plus Three.* Privately Printed. 1981.

Crook, George. *General George Crook: His Autobiography.* Edited by Martin F. Schmitt. Norman: University of Oklahoma Press, 1960.

Cullum, George W. *Biographical Register of the Officers and Graduates of the U.S. Military Academy at West Point, N.Y.,* 2 Volumes. New York: D. Van Nostrand, 1868.

De Barthe, Joe *The Life and Adventures of Frank Grouard,* Reprinted by Buffalo Bulletin, Buffalo Wyoming. No Date.

Dyer, Frederick. *A Compendium of the War of the Rebellion,* 3 Volumes. New York: Thomas Yoseloff, 1959.

Finerty, John F. *War-Path and Bivouac,* Lincoln: University of Nebraska Press, 1975.

Gray, John S. *Centennial Campaign: The Sioux War of 1876.* Fort Collins, Colorado: Old Army Press, 1976.

Greene, Jerome A. *Slim Buttes, 1876.* Norman: University of Oklahoma Press, 1982.

Grinnell, George Bird. *The Cheyenne Indians Their History and Ways of Life.* New York: Cooper Square Publishers, 1962.

———.*Fighting Cheyennes.* Norman: University of Oklahoma Press, 1955.

Hutchins, James S. *Boots and Saddles at the Little Bighorn.* Fort Collins, Colorado: Old Army Press, 1976.

Hutton, Paul A. *Phil Sheridan and his Army.* Lincoln: University of Nebraska Press, 1985.

John Stands In Timber and Liberty, Margot. *Cheyenne Memories.* New Haven: Yale University Press, 1967.

Johnson, Robert U. and Clarence C. Buell, editors. *Battles and Leaders,* 4 Volumes. New York: Thomas Yoseloff, 1956.

Johnson, Virginia Weigel. *The Unregimented General: A Biography of Nelson A. Miles.* Boston: Houghton Mifflin, 1962.

Knight, Oliver. *Following the Indian Wars: The Story of the Newspaper Correspondents Among the Indian Campaigners.* Norman: University of Oklahoma Press, 1960.

Linderman, Frank. *Plenty Coups, Chief of the Crows.* Lincoln: University of Nebraska Press, 1962.

Marquis, Thomas B. *Cheyennes of Montana*. Algonac, Michigan: Reference Publications, Inc., 1978.

———. *Wooden Leg: A Warrior Who Fought Custer*. Lincoln: University of Nebraska Press, 1976.

Marshall, S.L.A. *Crimsoned Prairie*. New York: Charles Scribner's Sons, 1972.

Mattes, Merrill J. *Indians, Infants and Infantry: Andrew and Elizabeth Burt On the Frontier*. Denver: Old West Publishing Co., 1960.

Miles, Nelson A. *Nelson A. Miles*, Brian Pohanka, editor. Glendale: Arthur H. Clark Co., 1985.

Mills, Anson. *My Story*. C.H. Claudy, editor. Washington, D.C.: Byron S. Adams, 1921.

Neihardt, John G. *Black Elk Speaks: Being the Life Story of a Holy Man of the Oglala Sioux*. Lincoln: University of Nebraska Press, 1965.

Porter, Joseph C. *Paper Medicine Man: John Gregory Bourke and His American West*. Norman: University of Oklahoma Press, 1986.

Powell, Peter J. *Sweet Medicine: The Continuing Role of the Sacred Arrows, the Sun Dance, and the Sacred Buffalo Hat in Northern Cheyenne History*, 2 Volumes. Norman: University of Oklahoma Press, 1969.

Sandoz, Mari. *Crazy Horse, the Stange Man of the Oglalas*. Lincoln, University of Nebraska Press, 1978.

Stackpole, Edward J. *Sheridan in the Shenandoah*. Harrisburg: Stackpole Co., 1961.

Stewart, Edgar I. *Custer's Luck*. Norman: University of Oklahoma Press, 1955.

Treholm, Virginia Cole, and Carley, Maurine. *The Shoshonis: Sentinels of the Rockies*. Norman: University of Oklahoma Press, 1964.

Utley, Robert M. *Frontier Regulars: The United States Army and the Indian, 1866-1891*. New York: Macmillan, 1973.

Vaughn, J.W. *Indian Fights: New Facts on Seven Encounters*. Norman: University of Oklahoma Press, 1966.

———. *The Reynolds Campaign on Powder River*. Norman: University of Oklahoma Press, 1961.

———. *With Crook at the Rosebud*. Harrisburg, Stackpole Co., 1956.

Vestal, Stanley. *Sitting Bull, Champion of the Sioux*. Norman: University of Oklahoma Press, 1957.

———. *Warpath and Council Fire: The Plains Indians' Struggle for Survival in War and in Diplomacy*. New York: Random House, 1948.

Warner, Ezra. *Generals in Blue*. Baton Rouge: Louisiana State University Press, 1964.

Werner, Fred. *Before the Little Big Horn*. Billings: Privately Printed, 1980.

———. *The Soldiers are Coming*. Greeley, Colorado: Werner Publications, 1982.

Willert, James. *Little Big Horn Diary*. La Mirada, California. Privately Printed, 1977.

Index

Index